Standards for Adult Education ESL Programs

Teachers of English to Speakers of Other Languages, Inc.

Typeset in Bodoni and Stone Serif
by Capitol Communication Systems, Inc., Crofton, Maryland USA
Printed by Kirby Lithographic Company, Inc., Arlington, Virginia, USA

Teachers of English to Speakers of Other Languages, Inc.
700 South Washington Street, Suite 200
Alexandria, Virginia 22314 USA
Tel 703-836-0774 • Fax 703-836-6447 • E-mail tesol@tesol.org • http://www.tesol.org/

Developed by the TESOL Task Force on Adult Education Program Standards:

Gretchen Bitterlin, Centers for Education and Technology, San Diego Community College District, San Diego, California
Marianne Dryden, Foreign Language Education, Department of Curriculum and Instruction, University of Texas, Austin, Texas
Holly Fadden, Maryland State Department of Education, Baltimore, Maryland
Leann Howard, Centers for Education and Technology, San Diego Community College District, San Diego, California
Susan Huss-Lederman, University of Wisconsin, Whitewater, Wisconsin
Autumn Keltner, Comprehensive Adult Student Assessment System (CASAS), San Diego, California
Margaret Kiernan, Virginia Beach Adult Learning Center, Virginia Beach, Virginia
Maria Koonce, Broward County Schools, Fort Lauderdale, Florida
Suzanne Leibman, College of Lake County, ESL Adult and Community Education, Grayslake, Illinois
Diane Pecoraro, Minnesota Department of Children, Families and Learning, Roseville, Minnesota
Joy Kreeft Peyton, National Center for ESL Literacy Education, Center for Applied Linguistics, Washington, DC
Kathleen Santopietro Weddel, Northern Colorado State Literacy Resource Center, Greeley, Colorado
Paula Schlusberg, New Readers Press, Syracuse, New York
Linda Taylor, Comprehensive Adult Student Assessment System (CASAS), Ridgefield Park, New Jersey
Carol Van Duzer, National Center for ESL Literacy Education, Center for Applied Linguistics, Washington, DC
Dan Wann, Indianapolis Public Schools, Division of Adult Education, Indianapolis, Indiana

Director of Communications and Marketing: Helen Kornblum
Managing Editor: Marilyn Kupetz
Additional Reader: Marcia Annis
Cover Design: Capitol Communication Systems, Inc.

All names of individuals are pseudonyms or are used with permission.

Every effort has been made to contact the copyright holders for permission to reprint borrowed material. We regret any oversights that may have occurred and will rectify them in future printings of this work.

ISBN 1-931185-03-4
Library of Congress Control No. 2002105951

Table of Contents

Acknowledgments v

Preface vii

Part 1: Introduction 1

Background of the Project 3

Goals of the Task Force 4

Core Definitions 4

Adult English Learners and Programs 5

Considerations Affecting the Development of Standards 8

Purpose and Uses of This Volume 10

  How to Score a Program Using the Program Self-Review Instrument 11

  Summary Scores and Action Plan Chart 16

  How to Use the Results 16

Part 2: Standards for Adult Education ESL Programs 17

1. Standards for Program Structure, Administration, and Planning 19
2. Standards for Curriculum and Instructional Materials 20
3. Standards for Instruction 20
4. Standards for Learner Recruitment, Intake, and Orientation 21
5. Standards for Learner Retention and Transition 22
6. Standards for Assessment and Learner Gains 22

7. Standards for Employment Conditions and Staffing 23

8. Standards for Professional Development and Staff Evaluation 23

9. Standards for Support Services 24

Part 3: Program Narratives 25

Introduction 27

Program 1: Large, Institution-Based Program 27

Narrative 27

Self-Review Instrument Samples 34

Summary Scores and Action Plan 36

Discussion of Scores for Program 1 42

Program 2: Volunteer-Based Program 43

Narrative 43

Self-Review Instrument Samples 47

Summary Scores and Action Plan 50

Discussion of Scores for Program 2 56

Part 4: Program Self-Review Instrument 59

Summary Scores and Action Plan Chart 143

Appendix: Educational Functioning Level Descriptors and Outcome Measure Definitions for Adult Basic Education and English as a Second Language 151

References and Further Reading 157

Acknowledgments

TESOL thanks the following people for their tireless efforts in making this publication a reality:

Project Coordinator: Gretchen Bitterlin

TESOL Task Force on Adult Education Program Standards Members: Marianne Dryden, Holly Fadden, Laureen Fredella, Leann Howard, Susan Huss-Lederman, Autumn Keltner, Margaret Kiernan, Maria Koonce, Suzanne Leibman, Diane Pecoraro, Joy Kreeft Peyton, Kathleen Santopietro Weddel, Paula Schlusberg, Linda Taylor, Carol Van Duzer, Dan Wann

Project Advisor: Joyce Campbell, Division of Adult Education and Literacy, U.S. Department of Education

TESOL Board Liaisons: Constantine Ioannou and Gail Weinstein
TESOL Staff Liaison: John Segota

Preface

What are the components of a quality adult education ESL program?

This volume attempts, for the first time on a national level, to answer this question by describing standards for program quality in nine areas:

1. program structure, administration, and planning
2. curriculum and instructional materials
3. instruction
4. learner recruitment, intake, and orientation
5. learner retention and transition
6. assessment and learner gains
7. employment conditions and staffing
8. professional development and staff evaluation
9. support services

Developed by a diverse task force of adult education ESL teachers, program administrators, and researchers from all over the United States, these standards reflect the great variety of adult ESL programs in the United States. The sample measures in the self-review instrument also provide a variety of ways to measure continuous improvement in small and large programs, something that is required by the Adult Education and Family Literacy Act of 1998 (H.R. 1385, Pub. L. No. 105-220). This volume will also be useful to adult education program directors or agencies setting up new ESL programs or reviewing existing programs.

This is a four-part volume. Part 1 describes the issues to be considered in developing standards for program quality and explains how to use the self-review instrument. Part 2 lists the standards. Part 3 describes two programs and demonstrates how they are scored on sample standards. Part 4 is a program self-review instrument that accompanies these standards. It contains specific descriptive examples of the standards in a variety of program types and a scoring guide for measuring implementation.

Part 1

Introduction

Part 1

Introduction

María, an outreach worker at a community center, notices that many of the parents who bring their children to the center have difficulty speaking English and filling out the registration forms. She would like to develop a program to help these adults learn English. She finds a local foundation willing to fund adult literacy programs, but she has no experience obtaining funding and would like some guidance on how to develop a strong program and apply for funding.

Diana and DiRonne are part-time teachers in a community college adult education program that offers courses in English to speakers of other languages (ESL). Their salaries are half the size of their part-time colleagues in the English department, but their classes are twice as large. In addition, they have been told that their photocopying budget has been cut and that the testing center on campus has eliminated adult education placement testing. Diana and DiRonne have been invited to join a program review committee for the college's accreditation review. They feel that these program structure and budget concerns should be documented and addressed, but they are not sure how to do so.

Reuben and Sarah are ESL specialists in their state's adult education division. The division recently sent applications for funding under the federal government's Workforce Investment Act to administrators of programs throughout the state that serve English language learners at the beginning levels. Reuben and Sarah have begun receiving phone calls from these administrators requesting information on how to document their learners' performance, according to the funding requirements. Reuben and Sarah would like to help these administrators identify effective means of tracking and documenting this performance.

The standards described in this volume are designed to assist professionals like these, who serve in a range of capacities related to adult education ESL programs in the United States.

Background of the Project

The Adult Education and Literacy Act of 1991 required adult basic education (ABE) programs in all states to develop indicators of program quality. The U.S. Department of Education provided examples of quality indicators for ABE programs in general but did not provide examples specifically related to adult education ESL programs (Office of Vocational and Adult Education, 1992). Therefore, in 1996, Teachers of English to Speakers of Other Languages, Inc. (TESOL)—the international association dedicated to developing the expertise of ESL professionals—appointed the Task Force on Adult Education Program Standards to review the accountability requirements in federal adult education legislation, existing program quality indicators from all states, and indicators previously written by TESOL.

After the first year, the task force concluded that there needed to be a new document specifically identifying standards for adult education ESL programs, according to the newer categories established by the U.S. Department of Education. Hence, in 1997, TESOL passed a resolution authorizing the task force to write new standards of program quality, with a process for measuring the extent to which those standards have been reached. The Workforce Investment Act of 1998 (H.R. 1385, Pub. L. No. 105-220) incorporated the Adult Education and Family Literacy Act, under which ABE, including ESL, is funded. This act not only requires states to continue to develop measures of program quality, but also requires the presentation of evidence of effective performance. Thus, the TESOL task force was positioned to provide examples of ways in which programs could meet the requirements of the federal legislation as well as local goals and needs.

Goals of the Task Force

Because adult education ESL programs across the United States are so diverse, the task force concluded that it would be impossible to write specific performance standards that would apply to all programs. Therefore, the task force revised its mission and decided to write overall standards of program quality, accompanied by sample measures and evidence of implementation of those measures, to serve as examples of what states could include in their own standards documents.

This volume identifies key criteria for a quality adult education ESL program—the standards—and the means by which to measure successful implementation of these standards—the measures of quality and the evidence. The goal of the task force, and the intent of these standards, is to provide a descriptive framework for examining any adult education ESL program. The standards are not meant to be prescriptive and should not be taken as such. Rather, they should provide individuals and communities with a starting point from which to begin adapting and implementing programs to fit local goals and needs.

Core Definitions

The following core definitions and concepts frame the development and use of these standards.

Adult Education ESL Programs

Adult education ESL programs are those programs in the United States that serve adults whose first language (L1) is not English. The primary objective of these programs is to enable adult learners who are not fully fluent and literate in English to become competent in communicating in English. This includes acquiring listening and speaking skills and the ability to read and write in English. These programs are designed to help these adults learn these skills so that they can meet their personal, vocational, academic, community, and employment goals. The great diversity in adult education ESL programs is discussed below and illustrated in two program narratives.

Literacy and ESL Literacy

In general, the term *literacy,* as used in this volume, is defined in the Adult Education and Family Literacy Act (Title II of the Workforce Investment Act of 1998; H.R. 1385, 1998) as "an individual's ability to read, write, and speak in English, compute and solve problems at levels of proficiency necessary to function on the job, in the family of the individual, and in society" (n.p.). In this definition, the phrase "in English" is key to the instruction of adult English learners. Even though adults may be literate—even highly educated—in their native language, they would still be included in the scope of this definition, because they still need to acquire

English language skills (listening, speaking, reading, and writing) that are traditionally thought of as literacy skills.

Given this definition, virtually any adult education ESL program could be called an ESL literacy program, but within adult ESL programs, the term *ESL literacy* refers to instruction specifically for English language learners who may not be fully literate in their native language—that is, they have limited or no reading and writing skills in their native language. In such cases, ESL literacy learners "may have acquired some conversational skills in English," but they have not necessarily acquired the reading and writing skills necessary "for access to training, job mobility, or success in regular ESL classes" (Wrigley, 1993, p. 1).

Differences Between Adult Education ESL and Adult Basic Education

In trying to identify what adult ESL education is, it is helpful to compare it with ABE and highlight the differences so that educators working with adult English learners can be responsive to their needs (see Burt & Cunningham Florez, 2001; Cunningham Florez & Burt, 2001). Although for federal and state funding purposes, adult ESL education is often treated as a category of ABE, adult English learners are very different from learners in ABE classes. The focus for the majority of ABE learners is acquisition of basic skills in reading, writing, and math. However, adult English learners who have already mastered these basic skills in their native language need to focus on the acquisition of a new language, including listening and speaking skills.

Of course, there are still many adult English learners in the United States who do not have a high school diploma either from their own country or from the United States (Kim, Collins, & McArthur, 1997). These learners need to improve their basic skills as do native speakers of English, but they need to be taught in different ways and with different materials than would be appropriate for teaching native English speakers. Learners in ABE classes use their mother tongue, English, to improve basic skills, gain knowledge, handle learning tasks, and communicate with teachers. Adult English learners, in contrast, may struggle to cope with oral and written directions, understand conversations laced with idiomatic language, and master not only the language of educational materials but also the culture on which those materials are based.

Adult English Learners and Programs

Adult English learners are a broadly diverse group, representing a wide range of linguistic, cultural, and educational backgrounds as well as ages and motivations for learning. The term *adult education ESL program* similarly encompasses great diversity of providers, types of programs, and program characteristics. To understand the standards presented in this volume, one must understand and take into account this great variety (see, e.g., National Center for ESL Literacy Education, 1998).

Characteristics of Adult English Learners

The population of adult English learners for whom these standards are written is very diverse but generally has the following characteristics:

- Adult English learners are 16 years old or older. A national study of new participants in federally funded adult education ESL programs found that 61% were under 31 years of age (National Center for ESL Literacy Education, 1999). In any one class, however, ages may range from 16 to 95. Adult ESL learners include permanent residents of the United States, immigrants, refugees, and migrant workers (Office of Vocational and Adult Education, 2000) coming from a variety of linguistic and cultural backgrounds. Although certain nationalities and language backgrounds may dominate in specific localities, wide diversity is very common. Any one ESL classroom may have many different language backgrounds represented.

- Adult English learners have a variety of educational backgrounds and literacy levels, from no education at all to advanced degrees. Again, looking at new participants in federally funded programs, one study indicated that half had at least a high school education, whereas 32% had fewer than 9 years of education. Of that 32%, 9% had fewer than 5 years of schooling (Fitzgerald, 1995; National Center for ESL Literacy Education, 1999). A study comparing literacy levels among adults in different countries found that in the United States, 64% of the foreign-born population speaking English as a second language scored at Level 1 (out of 5 levels) on the prose scale of the National Adult Literacy Survey (NALS), demonstrating "only rudimentary prose literacy skills, which makes it difficult to cope with the rising demands for literacy skills at work and in everyday life" (Tuijnman, 2000, p. 21). Other studies focusing specifically on participants in adult ESL literacy programs in the United States have found that most of these learners had only a few years of schooling, whether they came from literate societies, such as Mexico and El Salvador, or from preliterate societies, as in the case of the Hmong of Cambodia and Laos (Condelli & Wrigley, 2001; Wrigley, 1993). However, whatever their educational backgrounds, all adult English learners, in contrast to children, bring to the classroom a great deal of life experience and background knowledge from which to draw in their learning of English.

- Adult English learners are generally highly motivated and voluntarily enroll in ESL classes when they have time. They attend ESL classes for a variety of reasons, most predominantly because they desire to
    - learn English to communicate better in their everyday lives
    - get a job or improve their job status
    - become a citizen of the United States
    - get a high school diploma or GED (General Educational Development) certificate
    - acquire skills needed to advance to higher education programs (e.g., vocational training, college, university)
    - acquire skills to help their children succeed in school

(For discussion of these various reasons, see Kim, Collins, & McArthur, 1997; Stein, 1997; Terrill, 2000; Valentine, 1990.)

Some adults also attend in order to fulfill specially funded program requirements as a result of legislation, such as the Personal Responsibility and Work Opportunity Reconciliation Act of 1996.

The overriding common goal of all adult English learners is to make immediate use of their classroom learning in order to communicate with English speakers; learn about the culture and customs of the United States; and function effectively as individuals, family members, workers, community participants, and lifelong learners in the United States.

Providers and Types of Adult Education ESL Programs

Providers of adult education ESL programs are many and varied and include the following:

- **K–12 public school districts:** Many offer adult ESL instruction. In some public school programs, learners use the facilities of the K–12 divisions; in others, a dedicated facility under the auspices of the public school system is provided.
- **Community colleges:** Many also offer adult education ESL programs. Most community colleges do not charge tuition for these classes, although there may be fees for all or some classes.
- **Community-based organizations (CBOs):** CBOs, including volunteer-based programs, provide adult ESL instruction in many areas of the country and may act as the sole provider or may provide ancillary services to other programs. CBOs include literacy councils, religious-based organizations, ethnic organizations such as mutual assistance agencies (MAAs), and refugee service centers.
- **Correctional institutions:** Increasing numbers of correctional institutions provide adult education ESL programs, giving learners an opportunity to develop

language, life, and employment skills while serving their sentences.

- **Libraries:** In many areas, libraries are centers of adult ESL instruction, providing central locations, generally in close proximity to public transportation. A library may be the sponsor/provider of adult education ESL programs or may be the site for another provider's program. Many volunteer programs are library based, but not all library programs are operated and staffed by volunteers.
- **Workplaces:** Adult education ESL programs of several types are offered in many workplaces. These programs may be sponsored by a company, a union, a partnership of the two, or offered in collaboration with an educational institution. Services may be provided by the company, a union, or an educational institution with which the company contracts.

There are also many types of adult education ESL programs:

- **General English language development:** The majority of programs are those that deal with general English language development, focusing on reading, writing, listening, and speaking skills in all classes. These programs also assist learners in developing skills needed to survive in and adjust to many aspects of life in the United States, from shopping to preparing for a job to accessing health care.
- **Family ESL literacy:** In family ESL literacy programs, the family is the learning unit; instructional approaches center on families learning and using the new language together. These programs may focus particularly on meeting the goals of parents learning English in order to read to their children or help their children succeed in school in the United States. They aim to create a desire for lifelong learning and exemplify the idea that families provide an intergenerational transfer of language, traditions, and cultural values to their children. Components in family literacy include "interactive literacy activities between parents and their children, training for parents regarding how to be the primary teacher for their children, and parent literacy training that leads to economic self-sufficiency" (National Center for Family Literacy, 1999, p. 3).
- **Citizenship:** Citizenship preparation classes are an integral part of many programs, because some learners are seeking naturalization. Classes may offer English as part of preparation for full civic participation and empowerment, or they may focus solely on information and skills necessary to fulfill the naturalization requirements (National Institute for Literacy, 2001; Terrill, 2000).
- **Vocational ESL:** Vocational ESL (also referred to as VESOL or VESL) programs are designed to prepare learners for job training classes or employment in specific occupational areas. VESOL classes use job-related language and tasks as the vehicle for teaching English.
- **English for specific purposes:** English for specific purposes (ESP) focuses on developing the language and communication skills for professional fields of study, such as English for business, English for agriculture, or English for the medical field.
- **Workforce or workplace ESL:** Workforce or workplace ESL literacy programs focus on language and communication skills needed for success in the workplace. This type of program combines English language and literacy instruction with employment skills training. Workplace ESL classes are commonly supported by an employer and offered at a work site; they generally present a curriculum customized to the needs of the workers and the employer. The focus may be the skills needed for a particular job or workplace or more general skills.
- **Content-based ESL:** Content-based ESL concentrates on the subject matter that is being taught. The focus is on content, in which development of language skills is

embedded within the content instruction. Examples of content-based instruction include math for ESL learners or how to buy a home in the United States.

- **Preacademic ESL:** Preacademic ESL instruction concentrates on preparing learners for further education and training in postsecondary institutions, vocational education classes, or ABE and GED classes.

Characteristics of Adult Education ESL Programs

Programs serving adult ESL learners are as varied as the learners themselves. As the discussion of program types and providers above indicates, "diversity is the hallmark of ESL literacy programs" (Wrigley, 1993, p. 2). Adult education ESL programs are established in a variety of settings. Most common is the traditional classroom, but that classroom may be located at a work site, union hall, prison, or housing project, as well as in a school or community college. Literacy organizations and volunteer groups often provide one-to-one tutoring or instruction in very small groups. Learning labs, with computers, self-paced learning materials, and self-contained study packets are options being used in some areas to enhance learning. Distance learning in various modes, from video- to Internet-based models, is also being developed to provide greater flexibility for the large number of adult ESL learners needing educational services and, in some cases, to provide access to instruction when classrooms are limited.

Most adult education ESL programs offer a variety of scheduling options and arrangements, a flexibility designed to maximize learning opportunities and take into account the varied demands on learners' lives. Many programs offer open-entry/open-exit policies. Along with many day programs, evening programs are very common. The length of programs also varies, depending on factors ranging from funding requirements to the independently determined calendar of a host institution to the needs and desires of the group of learners. There is an increasing demand from a variety of sources, such as employers or human service agencies, for short-term and content-specific courses to meet specific performance outcomes.

The level of resources—physical and financial—available for adult education ESL programs also varies greatly. Funding comes from a wide range of public and private sources. Public money primarily comes through state and local agencies. Programs may also receive federal funds under the Workforce Investment Act of 1998. Program funding may also come from corporations, foundations, and, for some types of programs, private donations. Funding is often short term, and program personnel must constantly reapply and search for new sources of funds. Some programs serve populations that qualify for different funding streams, and administrators must juggle distinct requirements for use of funds as well as for reporting. Funding has a clear impact on a program's ability to provide facilities conducive to learning and quality instruction. Many programs are housed in facilities unsuitable for fostering learning; some even take place in temporary or makeshift facilities. A common challenge is teaching multilevel classes, usually with large numbers of learners and severely limited supplies. There are, of course, many other programs that are well funded, operating in facilities that support learning, with up-to-date equipment such as computers or other technology, and all necessary supplies. These well-funded facilities can and should serve as models for what is required for a quality adult education ESL program.

Considerations Affecting the Development of Standards

The standards in this volume represent underlying principles of adult learning and second language acquisition and the many factors affecting the acquisition of English by adult learners.

Adult Learning and Second Language Acquisition

Quality ESL programs for adults are very different from ESL programs for children and from programs teaching English to native English speakers. The following considerations from research in second language acquisition (SLA) and adult learning theory underlie many of the program standards.

Research in SLA tells us that adults and children differ to some degree in aspects of second language (L2) development. For example, the speed at which children and adults learn an L2 differs, with adolescents learning the quickest, followed by adults, and then children. Perhaps adult learners have more opportunities than children do to negotiate meaning in the additional language or have better developed cognitive abilities (Ellis, 1994). Children, on the other hand, normally acquire nativelike pronunciation of an L2, whereas adults generally do not, although, to date, there is no conclusive explanation for why this is the case (see Nunan, 1999, for a summary of related research).

Although little SLA research has been conducted on the relationship between literacy in the L1 and acquisition of an L2, research in learning strategies and L2 learning does indicate that, among children and teenagers, transfer of academic literacy skills learned through one language to academic contexts in an L2 is not automatic (O'Malley & Chamot, 1990). Imagine, then, the considerable challenges facing adult ESL learners who have received little to no schooling in their native language or who come from a preliterate society.

The learning of adult English learners, as for all L2 learners, is facilitated when instruction integrates the language skills (e.g., speaking, listening, reading, writing) when appropriate, providing a textured, rich experience in which skills reinforce each other in the learning process (Brown, 1994). Research indicates that adults learn best when learning is contextualized, emphasizing communication of meaning and use of English in real situations. Furthermore, by drawing on learners' background knowledge and valuing the experiences that adult learners bring to the classroom, adult education ESL programs can make instruction more relevant to the learners, who have limited time to devote to formal learning.

Factors Affecting the Acquisition of English by Adult English Learners

One of the most commonly asked questions of professionals in the field of adult education ESL is how long it takes speakers of other languages to learn English. This question comes not only from the learners themselves but also from sponsors, employers, school officials, friends, and family members. Although there is no single or absolute answer, research and experience indicate that learning a second language takes a considerable period of time. It is generally accepted that it takes from 5 to 7 years to move from not knowing any English to being able to accomplish most communication tasks including academic tasks" (Collier, 1989; National Center for ESL Literacy Education, 1999). The Mainstream English Language Project (MELT), conducted in the 1980s, identified 10 Student Performance Levels (SPLs) on a scale of no proficiency to fluency equal to that of a native English speaker. Field testing for that project at various programs in the United States indicated that a range of 120 to 235 hours of study may be needed for an individual learner to move up one SPL (Grognet, 1997). Most adults do not have much time to devote to learning the language, yet they need to acquire a functional use of English as soon as possible. Opportunities to use English outside the classroom constitute one factor that can decrease the time it takes for the adult English learner to attain functional skills and even fluency.

The wide range of time estimates for developing English language skills reflects the variety of factors that affect the rate at which an adult will learn English in the United States. These factors include the program characteristics described above and, in particular, the great variety of learner characteristics.

The age of the learner plays a significant role in English language learning. Younger adults often tend to learn English more quickly than older adults. With the wide mix of ages in many classes, the difference in ability to acquire new language skills may be particularly apparent and create additional instructional challenges.

Language background may also affect learning. Learners whose language does not use the Roman alphabet may need more time than those whose language shares an alphabet and vocabulary base with English.

Level of prior education plays a significant role in speed of language acquisition. Learners with higher levels of education commonly progress more quickly than those with more limited education (see Comprehensive Adult Student Assessment System, 1999).

The degree of L1 literacy is another important factor affecting acquisition of English, particularly reading and writing skills. Adult English learners who have limited or no literacy skills in their native language face additional learning challenges as they grapple with initial literacy development along with a new language.

Cultural background also comes into play. For example, some adult English learners are not accustomed to being taught by a member of the opposite sex and need time to adjust to this situation. Others come from highly formal, teacher-centered classrooms and find the informality of the U.S. classroom and the active participation of learners troublesome to the point of interfering with learning.

The culture shock experienced by adult ESL learners and the varied circumstances that brought such learners to the United States and to the class may affect learning as well. Often, the learners' emotional turmoil about, or even resistance to, being in the United States can block their language acquisition. Other emotional or psychological factors may also interfere. English learners may be dealing with loneliness, disorienting shifts in family structure, domestic violence, or posttraumatic stress disorder (see Isserlis, 2000).

For some adult English learners, learning and access to an educational program is affected by a condition, such as a learning disability, visual or auditory impairment, or other physical impairment requiring adaptation of equipment, environment, or manner of instruction (see Schwarz & Terrill, 2000). These special needs may be more difficult to discern in English language learners than in native English speakers, and these learners may be less aware of their rights to accommodations under the law than persons who speak English or those who have lived in the United States longer. Ideally, to enhance access and educational opportunities for these special needs learners, program designs should include recruiting materials and methods for serving visually or hearing impaired persons, registration and placement processes that accommodate all kinds of learners, and personnel at all levels who are aware of the special needs of these learners and can adapt instruction to suit those needs.

Motivational factors—the reasons for which learners come to an ESL program—can also affect acquisition of English. Externally imposed requirements, such as recent abrupt changes in citizenship or welfare legislation, are likely to create emotional turmoil that can interfere with learning. Personal goals, such as the desire to help one's children with schoolwork or improve one's job performance, can stimulate acquisition when the learning is clearly directed toward achieving those goals.

The personal situation of adult learners and the many demands on their lives affect attendance in class and the amount of time they have to devote to learning English. Many issues can interfere with an individual's ability to focus on learning:

- work demands, including long hours, split shifts, and changing schedules
- family responsibilities, including child and elder care
- overall health and well-being of the learner
- access to an adult education ESL program, including availability of transportation and childcare

In short, because of their varied backgrounds and experiences, adult English learners learn in a variety of ways and progress at different rates. This means that there is no single method of language instruction that is appropriate for all adult English learners, and there are no exact time lines identifying how long it may take an adult learner to acquire fluency in English.

Purpose and Uses of This Volume

The standards provided here are not intended to create prescriptive or rigid requirements for all adult education ESL programs. Rather, they are written to be of use with many different types of programs. Due to the variation among programs and learners, implementation or use of the standards must take into account issues such as program size, autonomy, goals, funding requirements and restrictions, learner goals and characteristics, program resources, staffing, and many other factors. The impact of this variation means that, in some cases, a particular standard or standards cannot, and should not, be applied to a particular program.

This volume can be used by a variety of individuals for different purposes. If a program is undergoing accreditation review, all program staff (including administrators, teachers, and support staff) as well as external reviewers might complete all of the self-review instrument sheets, or different groups might complete different sheets, with the goal of reviewing implementation of all of the standards. If a program wants to review only one component (e.g., effectiveness of instruction), those staff involved in that aspect of the program might review only that section of the standards.

This volume consists of a set of 82 standards, divided into nine categories (Part 2). These are followed by descriptions of two adult education programs, to give program staff a sense of how these standards might be implemented in a large school-based adult education program and in a small volunteer program (Part 3). These two programs are not meant to represent model or ideal programs but rather real programs in which some standards are well in place, others are not, and others are in place to some extent.

Following each program description, the program is scored on the self-review instrument to provide an example of how the self-review instrument can be used.

Part 4 contains the Program Self-Review Instrument. In this instrument, each program quality standard or group of standards has a separate self-review sheet. This sheet contains the statement of the standard, the measures to determine the degree of implementation of the standard, and samples of evidence showing that this standard is in place.

How to Score a Program Using the Program Self-Review Instrument

Once program staff have read the standard statement, they should do the following:

- Check the items on that sheet under Measures to indicate those that are in place in the program.
- List other measures if applicable.
- Check the Sample Evidence of implementation of those measures.
- List additional evidence if applicable.
- Write qualifying comments about the evidence as needed (e.g., some evidence may be in developmental stages, not fully implemented yet).
- Review the checks made next to the measures and the evidence.
- Assign a score for that standard as follows:
  - 3 — well developed
  - 2 — in place
  - 1 — somewhat in place or partially developed
  - 0 — not in place

If a given standard is not relevant to the program being reviewed, place NA (not applicable) in the score box. For example, a program may not formally conduct its own assessment of learners but rather work with other organizations to carry that out. In this case, Standard 6, E—The program provides appropriate facilities, equipment, and conditions for assessment activities—is not relevant, and NA is placed in the score box for that standard.

In the Measures section of the self-review instrument, criteria for a minimum score of 2 are defined in three different ways, depending on the standard. These criteria are given on each page of the self-review instrument. (See p. 12 for a thumbnail sketch of how to read the self-review instrument.)

For some standards, all of the measures listed should be in place for a minimum score of 2.

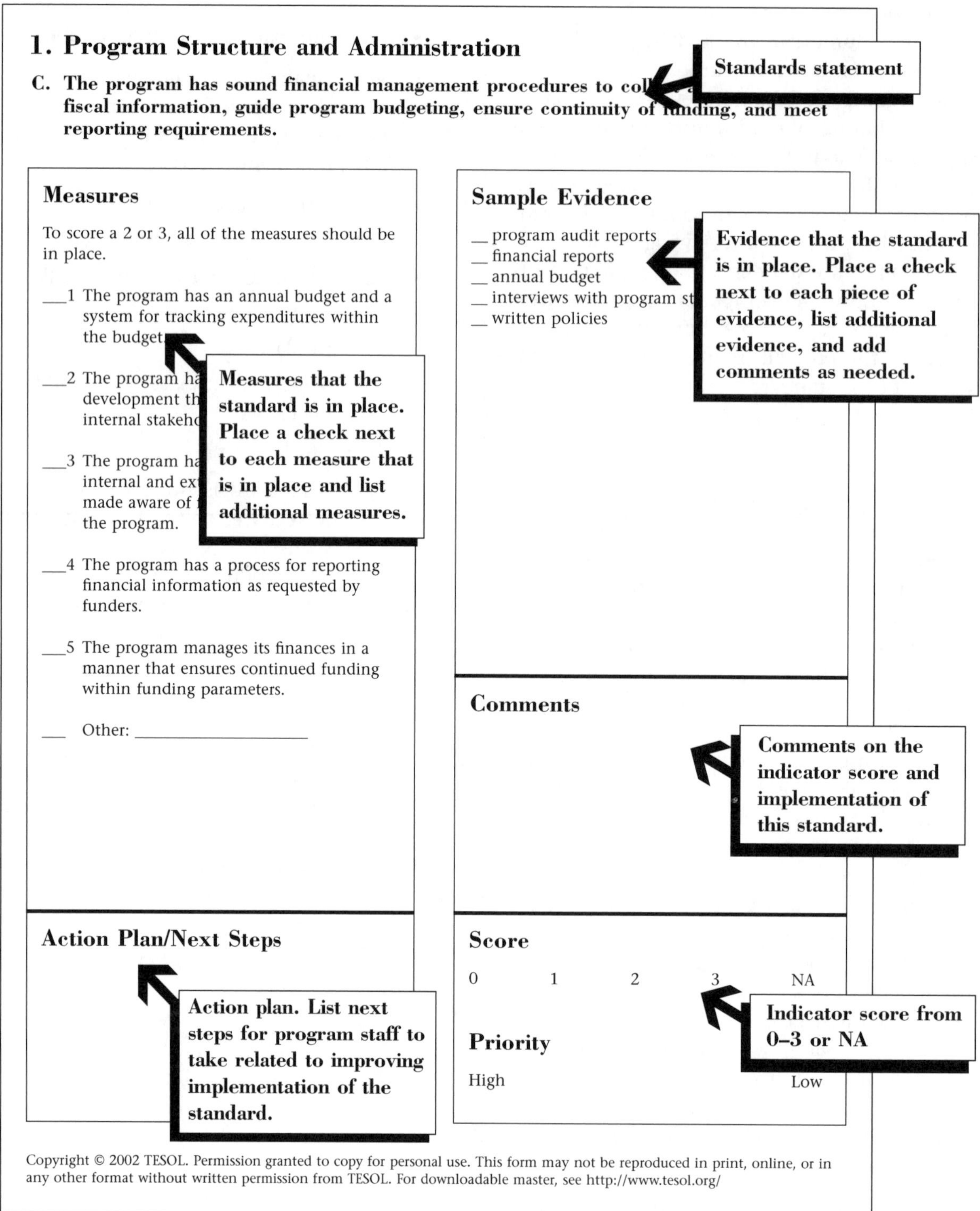

1. Program Structure and Administration

C. The program has sound financial management procedures to col[...] fiscal information, guide program budgeting, ensure continuity of [...]ding, and meet reporting requirements.

Measures

To score a 2 or 3, all of the measures should be in place.

___1 The program has an annual budget and a system for tracking expenditures within the budget.

___2 The program ha[...] development th[...] internal stakeho[...]

___3 The program ha[...] internal and ex[...] made aware of [...] the program.

___4 The program has a process for reporting financial information as requested by funders.

___5 The program manages its finances in a manner that ensures continued funding within funding parameters.

___ Other: ___________

Sample Evidence

__ program audit reports
__ financial reports
__ annual budget
__ interviews with program st[...]
__ written policies

Comments

Action Plan/Next Steps

Score

0 1 2 3 NA

Priority

High Low

For some standards, all of the measures marked with a * should be in place for a minimum score of 2.

2. Curriculum and Instructional Materials

F. The program has an ongoing process for curriculum revision in response to the changing needs of the learners, community, and policies.

Measures

To score a 2 or 3, all the * measures should be in place.

*__1 Curriculum is reviewed or revised in one or more of the following ways:

- __ Curriculum is reviewed as part of a formal program review process that is regularly scheduled.
- __ Curriculum emerges from participatory activities between learners and the instructor.
- __ Program funds or seeks funding for curriculum projects targeted to specific or changing needs (e.g., integration of technology competencies into course outlines, development of curriculum for new semiliterate population, development of curriculum to meet the requirements of legislation in order to acquire government funding).

*__2 As part of the review process, the program seeks input from internal and external stakeholders, as appropriate.

*__3 Faculty and staff contribute new curriculum materials to central resource area accessible to other instructors.

*__4 Textbook committee meets regularly to select and approve new materials.

*__5 The curriculum review process includes steps to disseminate the materials throughout the program.

Sample Evidence

__ needs assessments
__ guidelines for curriculum review
__ minutes of curriculum meetings (date of last review meeting: ___________)
__ questionnaires or surveys
__ telephone notes
__ lists of participants and contributors in curriculum review process
__ memos
__ meeting agendas
__ schedule for textbook committee meetings (date of most recent meeting: ________)
__ other:________________________

Comments

Action Plan/Next Steps

Score

0 1 2 3 NA

Priority

High Low

For some standards, one or more of the listed items should be in place for a minimum score of 2.

3. Instruction

C. Instructional activities engage the learners in taking an active role in the learning process.

Measures

To score a 2 or 3, the following measure should be in place.

___1 Learners take an active role in the learning process by doing one or more of the following:

- __ Learners complete exercises requiring active listening skills.
- __ Learners communicate with each other or the instructor on a regular basis in the classroom.
- __ Learners ask questions or request clarification in discussions or presentations.
- __ Learners revise and edit written assignments as part of the writing process.
- __ Learners engage in tasks in which they research information and then share it with others.
- __ Learners participate in the process of identifying course objectives.
- __ Learners have roles in class management tasks (e.g., helping new students).
- __ Learners document their own progress in meeting those objectives.

___ Other: ____________________

Sample Evidence

__ classroom observations
__ lesson plans
__ interviews with Instructors
__ interviews with learners
__ learner role assignments listed on charts
__ learner self-evaluations or portfolios
__ other: ____________________

Comments

Action Plan/Next Steps

Score

0 1 2 3 NA

Priority

High Low

As mentioned above, in the Measures section of the self-review instrument, criteria are given for assigning a minimum score of 2 or 3. The difference between a score of 2 or 3 relates to the extent to which the measures are implemented according to those rating the program components. For example, Standard I, under Program Structure and Administration, relates to "providing courses of sufficient intensity and duration with flexible schedules." The scoring sheet states that all the measures must be in place for a minimum score of 2 or 3. If program

1. Program Structure and Administration

I. The program provides courses of sufficient intensity and duration with flexible schedules to meet varied learner and community needs in convenient locations within the constraints of program resources.

Measures

To score a 2 or 3, all the measures should be in place.

___1 Based on learner needs, the program offers one or more of the following:

- __ classes of different duration (e.g., 6 weeks, 12 weeks, 18 weeks)
- __ classes at different times (e.g., mornings, afternoons, evenings, weekends)
- __ classes at different locations (e.g., school, institution, church, mobile van, library, workplace)
- __ distance-learning options (e.g., check-out of videos, Internet-based classes, telecourses)

___2 The program has a process to periodically review learner needs related to the scheduling of instruction (e.g., student surveys, community surveys, student focus groups).

____ Other: ____________________

Sample Evidence

- __ survey results
- __ class schedules
- __ interviews with program staff
- __ flyers and advertisements showing course locations
- __ meeting minutes
- __ program reports
- __ Web sites
- __ needs assessments or surveys
- __ focus group notes
- __ distance-learning materials
- __ other: ____________________

Comments

Action Plan/Next Steps

Score

0 1 2 3 NA

Priority

High Low

reviewers determine that the program does have all the required measures in place (e.g., courses of different lengths and in different locations), but they also know that there could be much more variety in program scheduling and that program staff have not surveyed learners recently to determine their course scheduling needs, they might assign a score of 2 for the standard instead of 3.

Similarly, under Employment Conditions, if some teachers had benefits, but the majority did not, the standard would likely not be given a 3, because there would be room for considerable improvement in the implementation of those measures by increasing the number of instructional staff with benefits. In summary, the degree to which measures are in place in terms of frequency of occurrence or quality of implementation determines whether a standard would receive a score of 2 or 3.

When a score has been assigned, comments can be written and an action plan outlined.

Summary Scores and Action Plan Chart

The summary scoring chart allows a review of the scores on all of the standards. On that chart, fill in the score given for each standard and add up the scores for an overall score for the section. The information from this chart should give program staff a good idea of which program components are in place and where program improvement efforts should be focused.

How to Use the Results

The results of this review can be used in different ways for program development and improvement. For instance, María, the outreach worker at the community center who wants to set up an ESL program for parents, can identify the important components of such a program by using the standards to develop a program development plan and to justify the level of funding that she requests.

Diana and DiRonne, the part-time teachers who serve on a program review committee at their community college, can use the standards as criteria for analyzing the strengths and weaknesses of their program and to set up an action plan for program improvement. The standards supporting equitable compensation for staff, placement testing, and appropriate class size are a few examples of criteria they can use to develop an ESL program review self-study instrument for accreditation purposes.

Reuben and Sarah, working in their state's department of education, can use the standards on assessment and learner gains, and their related measures, to advise administrators or program directors who need to write local performance measures as required by their state plan.

María, Diane, DiRonne, Reuben, and Sarah represent the thousands of people in the field of adult education whose main goal is to provide quality ESL instruction for adult learners. We hope that this volume serves as a useful tool in that endeavor.

Part 2

Standards for Adult Education ESL Programs

Part 2

Standards for Adult Education ESL Programs

1. Standards for Program Structure, Administration, and Planning

Program Structure and Administration

A. The program has a mission statement, a clearly articulated philosophy, and goals developed with input from internal and external stakeholders.

B. The program has an administrative system (e.g., board of directors or advisory group and bylaws) that ensures participation of internal stakeholders, accountability, and effective administration of all program activities. (The system of governance will vary according to whether the program is autonomous or affiliated with a larger institution or organization.)

C. The program has sound financial management procedures to collect and maintain fiscal information, guide program budgeting, ensure continuity of funding, and meet reporting requirements.

D. The program has an accountability plan with a system for record keeping and reporting that is consistent with program policies and legal and funding requirements.

E. The program fosters and maintains linkages and clear communication with internal and external stakeholders.

F. The program has a procedure for ensuring confidentiality in communication with internal and external stakeholders.

G. The program provides equipment for daily operations and efficient record keeping.

H. The program uses facilities and resources appropriate for adult ESL instruction, meeting the needs of learners and instructional staff. If a program is part of a larger institution, facilities meet standards equivalent to those of other programs.

I. The program provides courses of sufficient intensity and duration with flexible schedules to meet varied learner and community needs in convenient locations within the constraints of program resources.

J. The program maintains a learner-teacher ratio conducive to meeting learning needs and goals.

K. The program has a curriculum, including learning goals, materials, and resources, for each type of instructional offering. (See 2.

Standards for Curriculum and Instructional Materials.)

L. The program organizes its instructional offerings to be consistent with the program's mission and goals and with the goals and needs of learners in the community being served. (See 3. Standards for Instruction.)

M. The program has a comprehensive assessment and evaluation policy and procedures that link assessment to instruction as well as learner goals and needs. (See 6. Standards for Assessment and Learner Gains.)

N. The program supports employment conditions, compensation, and benefits commensurate with those of other instructional or professional staff with comparable qualifications (e.g., the program employs full-time instructional staff and provides part-time teachers with prorated benefits). (See 7. Standards for Employment Conditions and Staffing.)

Program Planning

O. The program has a planning process for initial program development and ongoing program improvement that is guided by evaluation and based on a written plan that considers targeted community demographics, retention patterns, learner needs, resources, local economic trends, and educational and technological trends in the field.

P. The program has a technology plan that is aligned with program goals and learner needs. The plan addresses the use, acquisition, and maintenance of technological resources and the training of program personnel.

Q. The program has a plan for outreach, marketing, and public relations to foster awareness and understanding of the program.

2. Standards for Curriculum and Instructional Materials

A. The program has a process for developing curriculum that is based on a needs assessment of learners and includes participation and input from other stakeholders.

B. The curriculum reflects the mission and philosophy of the program and is compatible with principles of second language acquisition for adult learners.

C. The curriculum includes goals, objectives, outcomes, approaches, methods, activities, materials, technological resources, and evaluation measures that are appropriate for meeting learners' needs and goals.

D. The curriculum specifies measurable learning objectives for each instructional offering for learners and is appropriate for learners in multilevel classes.

E. The curriculum and instructional materials are easily accessible, up to date, appropriate for adult learners, culturally sensitive, oriented to the language and literacy needs of the learners, and suitable for a variety of learning styles.

F. The program has an ongoing process for curriculum revision in response to the changing needs of the learners, community, and policies.

3. Standards for Instruction

A. Instructional activities adhere to principles of adult learning and language acquisition. These principles include the following:

- Adult learners bring a variety of experiences, skills, and knowledge to the classroom that need to be acknowledged and included in lessons.
- Language acquisition is facilitated through providing a nonthreatening environment in which learners feel comfortable and self-confident and are encouraged to take risks to use the target language.
- Adult learners progress more rapidly when the content is relevant to their lives.
- Language learning is cyclical, not linear, so learning objectives need to be recycled in a variety of contexts.

B. Instructional approaches are varied to meet the needs of adult learners with diverse educational and cultural backgrounds. Examples of these approaches include, but are not limited to, the following:

- grammar-based (focus on the basic structure of language, e.g., grammar, vocabulary, and pronunciation)

- competency-based or functional context (focus on application of specific basic language skills in areas needed to function in everyday life or at work)
- whole language (integrated approach using listening, speaking, reading, and writing in thematic contexts often introduced through learner-generated content)
- participatory (focus on developing language and literacy skills to facilitate personal empowerment, community involvement, and social change)
- content-based (focus on developing language to support learner success in specific content areas, such as citizenship or vocational training)
- project-based (focus on developing language through collaborative work with the goal of completing a task or developing a product)

C. Instructional activities engage learners so that they take an active role in the learning process.

D. Instructional activities focus on the acquisition of communication skills necessary for learners to function within the classroom, outside the classroom, or in other educational programs (e.g., ABE, GED preparation, postsecondary education, vocational training programs).

E. Instructional activities integrate the four language skills (listening, speaking, reading, and writing), focusing on receptive and productive skills appropriate to learners' needs.

F. Instructional activities are varied to address the different learning styles (e.g., aural, oral, visual, kinesthetic) and special learning needs of the learners.

G. Instructional activities incorporate grouping strategies and interactive tasks that facilitate the development of authentic communication skills. These include cooperative learning, information gap activities, role plays, simulations, problem solving, and problem posing.

H. Instructional activities take into account the needs of multilevel groups of learners, particularly those with minimal literacy skills in their native language and English.

I. Instructional activities focus on the development of language and culturally appropriate behaviors needed for critical thinking, problem solving, team participation, and study skills.

J. Instructional activities give learners opportunities to use authentic resources both inside and outside the classroom (e.g., newspapers, telephone books, school notices, library resources, community agencies, work sites, television, and the Internet).

K. Instructional activities give learners opportunities to develop awareness of and competency in the use of appropriate technologies to meet lesson objectives.

L. Instructional activities are culturally sensitive to the learners and integrate language and culture.

M. Instructional activities prepare learners for formal and informal assessment situations, such as test taking, job interviews, and keeping personal learning records.

4. Standards for Learner Recruitment, Intake, and Orientation

A. A quality ESL program has effective procedures for identifying and recruiting adult English learners. The procedures include strategies for collecting data on community demographics that identify the populations that need to be served, particularly those at the lowest level of literacy and knowledge of English.

B. The program uses a variety of recruitment strategies (e.g., personal contacts, peer learner referrals, print and broadcast media, outreach to community groups, networking with various institutions, advertising through and participation in community events, use of technological sources such as Web sites and electronic discussion lists).

C. The program takes steps to ensure that culturally and linguistically appropriate recruitment and program information materials and activities reach the appropriate populations in multiple languages as needed. Recruitment materials suitable for persons with special needs are available (e.g., larger print, audiotapes).

D. The program evaluates the effectiveness of its recruitment efforts and makes changes as needed.

E. The program has an intake process that provides appropriate assessment of learners' needs, goals, and language proficiency levels; an orientation process that provides learners with information about the program; and, if needed, a procedure for referring learners to support services within the program or through other agencies and for accommodating learners waiting to enter the program.

5. Standards for Learner Retention and Transition

A. The program supports retention through enrollment and attendance procedures that reflect program goals, requirements of program funders, and demands on the adult learner (e.g., flexible enrollment options, flexible transfer, and short-term courses).

B. The program encourages learners to participate consistently and long enough to reach their identified goals. This may be accomplished by adjusting the scheduling and location of classes and by providing appropriate support services.

C. The program accommodates the special needs of learners as fully as possible.

D. The program contacts learners with irregular attendance patterns and acknowledges learners who attend regularly.

E. The program provides learners with appropriate support for transition to other programs (e.g., adult basic education (ABE), General Educational Development (GED) preparation, job training, postsecondary education) or to the workplace.

6. Standards for Assessment and Learner Gains

Assessment Policy

A. The program has a comprehensive assessment policy that reflects the mission and goals of the program; legal requirements; needs of the learners and other stakeholders; principles of adult learning, second language acquisition, language learning pedagogy, and literacy development for adults; and instructional objectives and activities.

B. The program has a process for assessing learners' skills and goals for placement into the program, documentation of progress within the program, and exit from the program. This includes appropriate assessment of learners with special learning needs.

C. Assessment activities are ongoing and appropriately scheduled.

D. The program has procedures for collecting and reporting data on educational gains and outcomes. Data are reported in clear and precise language to all stakeholders without violating standards of confidentiality.

E. The program provides appropriate facilities, equipment, supplies, and personnel for assessment activities (e.g., space for intake and initial assessment, sufficient audiovisual equipment).

Types of Assessment

F. The program identifies learners' needs and goals as individuals, family members, community participants, workers, and lifelong learners.

G. The program assesses the language proficiency levels of learners in the areas of listening, speaking, reading, and writing. The assessments may also identify learners' literacy skills in their primary language and any learning disabilities.

H. The program uses a variety of appropriate assessments, including authentic, performance-based assessments; standardized tests; learner self-assessment; and assessment of nonlinguistic outcomes (e.g., perceived improvement in self-esteem, participation in teamwork activities). Standardized assessment instruments are valid and reliable, based on studies with the targeted adult-level population.

Uses of Assessment

I. The information obtained through needs assessment is used to aid administrators, teachers, and tutors in developing curricula, materials, skills assessments, and teaching approaches that are relevant to learners' lives.

J. Assessment results are clearly explained and shared with learners, to the extent permitted by assessment guidelines, in order to help learners progress.

K. Assessment activities document learners' progress within the ESL program toward advancement to other training programs, employment, postsecondary education, and attainment of other educational goals.

L. Results of assessment provide information about educational gains and learner outcomes and provide the basis for recommendations for further assessment (e.g., special needs, literacy considerations).

Learner Gains

The program has a process by which the following are accomplished:

M. Learners identify and demonstrate progress toward or attainment of their short- and long-term goals.

N. Learners demonstrate skill-level improvements in listening, speaking, reading, and writing through a variety of assessments.

O. Learners demonstrate progress in nonlinguistic areas identified as important toward meeting their goals.

7. Standards for Employment Conditions and Staffing

Employment Conditions

A. The program supports compensation and benefits commensurate with those of instructional and other professional staff with comparable positions and qualifications within similar institutions.

B. The program has in place policies and procedures that ensure professional treatment of staff.

C. The program supports a safe and clean working environment.

Staffing

D. The program recruits and hires qualified instructional staff with training in the theory and methodology of teaching ESL. Qualifications may vary according to local agency requirements and type of instructional position (e.g., paid teacher, volunteer).

E. The program recruits and hires qualified administrative, instructional, and support staff who have appropriate training in cross-cultural communication, reflect the cultural diversity of the learners in the program, and have experience with or awareness of the specific needs of adult English learners in their communities.

F. The program recruits and hires qualified support staff to ensure effective program operation.

8. Standards for Professional Development and Staff Evaluation

Professional Development

A. The program has a process for orienting new ESL administrative, instructional, and support staff to the ESL program, its goals, and its learners.

B. The program has a professional development plan, developed with input from staff and stakeholders. The program acquires appropriate resources to implement the plan, including compensation for staff participation.

C. The program provides opportunities for its instructional staff to expand their knowledge of current trends, best practices, uses of technology, and research in the field of second language acquisition and adult literacy development.

D. The program provides opportunities for administrators and project evaluators to become knowledgeable about effective teaching strategies in adult ESL and current trends in the field of adult ESL.

E. Professional development activities are varied, based on needs of the staff, and provide opportunities for practice and consistent follow-up.

F. The program provides training in assessment procedures and in the interpretation and use of assessment results.

G. The program encourages faculty and staff to join professional ESL and adult education organizations and supports staff participation in professional development activities of the organizations.

H. The program supports collaboration among adult ESL teachers, instructional personnel in other content areas, K–12 English and ESL teachers, support service providers, workplace personnel, and representatives of programs to which learners transition.

I. The program has a process for recognizing the participation of staff in professional development activities.

Staff Evaluation

J. The program has a process for the regular evaluation of administrator, teacher, and support staff performance that is consistent with the program's philosophy. The process is developed with input from staff.

K. The program provides learners with opportunities to evaluate program staff anonymously. The tools are user friendly and allow for variety in learner proficiency levels, backgrounds, cultural diversity, and special needs.

L. The program provides opportunities for all staff members to develop performance improvement plans.

9. Standards for Support Services

A. The program provides students with access to a variety of services directly or through referrals to cooperating agencies.

B. The program provides a process for identifying learning disabilities in English language learners and incorporates appropriate accommodations and training of staff, either directly through the program or indirectly through referrals to cooperating agencies.

C. The program develops linkages with cooperating agencies to ensure that referrals to support services result in meeting learners' needs, including those of learners with disabilities.

Part 3

Program Narratives

Part 3

Program Narratives

Introduction

Because adult education ESL programs are so diverse, standards may be implemented in a variety of ways. The following descriptions of two sample adult education ESL programs—a large, school-based program and a small volunteer program—illustrate ways in which the standards outlined in this volume may be applied. These program narratives do not describe perfect programs, but rather sample programs with some well-developed program components and other components that are not so well developed.

Following each narrative are sample, scored self-review items for two standards that illustrate how the self-review instrument can be used to determine to what extent and in what ways the standards have been implemented. These are followed for each program by a chart of summary scores and an action plan for each section of standards to show how the program was scored on all the standards. This chart illustrates the program's overall strengths and areas in which improvement is needed. It allows program staff to look at the program as a whole and identify quickly the priority areas needing improvement.

Program 1: Large, Institution-Based Adult ESL Program

Narrative

Program Structure, Administration, and Planning

This sample ESL program (Program 1) is part of a noncredit community college program. ESL is one of the nine mandated programs offered at six centers in a large metropolitan continuing education program. The total ESL learner population served per year is approximately 30,000. The governance structure for the noncredit continuing education program consists of a president and vice president, and instructional deans and associate deans at each center who supervise the faculty and staff. Before administrators are hired they are interviewed by a hiring committee who inquires about their knowledge and experience in working with nonnative speakers of English.

Program 1 has a mission statement that is part of the school's master plan, a curriculum, assessment procedures, and a program review process. The program review process has not been in operation for a couple of years as the forms are being revised. To meet accreditation requirements and federal funding requirements, the program went through a self-study process last year. Whereas internal stakeholders were consulted, time was not devoted to seeking input from external stakeholders in this program review process.

The program is funded by the state according to average daily attendance, but also receives supplementary monies through the Federal Adult Education and Literacy Act.

An average class size of 25 is required to keep an ESL class open. If the average class size drops too low, the class is in danger of being closed. This requirement is a source of controversy in the program because on occasion classes that meet special needs (e.g., low literacy levels), are closed because of small class size.

The ESL program works cooperatively with the local unified school district, refugee resettlement agencies, literacy organizations, churches, and other community agencies to provide a wide variety of ESL programs in the community. Although some classes are held at the six main centers, numerous classes are held at off-site locations in the community, such as churches, recreation centers, and elementary schools. Classes are offered mornings, afternoons, and evenings at all the centers. Several centers offer Friday evening and Saturday morning classes. Although there is demand for more of these classes, limited funding prevents more of these classes from being opened. Several classes have waiting lists. At this time, there are no distance-learning options for ESL instruction. Enrollment is open entry, open exit in almost all classes. This provides easy access to ESL instruction for learners but affects instruction sometimes in a negative way.

The school makes sure that each classroom meets the criteria for appropriate facilities. Facilities are checked to make sure each classroom is clean, has appropriate tables and chairs, a white board or black board, and storage space for instructional materials. The six main centers also have workrooms where teachers can prepare their lessons. In most cases, the school provides an overhead projector and screen as well. Some classes at off-site locations do not have telephone access to the main center in case of an emergency, and this causes concern among some faculty.

The ESL program has conducted a survey to identify needs of its learners in computer literacy, but has not formulated a formal technology plan. The program is seeking grant monies to finance this development. In terms of marketing, there is an ESL representative on the district's marketing committee. Budget constraints do not allow for the support of some proposed marketing strategies for the ESL learner population such as radio ads in languages other than English.

Curriculum and Instructional Materials

The curriculum for this large, well-established, institutionally based adult ESL program was developed by a committee of ESL faculty and is revised periodically according to changing learner needs. Learner surveys are sometimes used to inform the program about needed changes. For example, in a recent survey, learners expressed interest in the integration of computer skills into their courses and options for distance learning. Based on the state's *Model Standards,* which were written in 1992, the curricular document consists of learning objectives for seven levels of instruction.

Each course outline includes goals, objectives, methods, recommended materials, evaluation measures, and instructional standards. Following a competency-based approach, the objectives define what learners will be able to do with the language upon completion of the objectives. In addition to general competencies in the areas of listening, speaking, reading, and writing for each level, there are content objectives on topics such as personal identification, health, transportation, housing, and shopping for each level of instruction. Each outline also lists functions and grammatical forms for each level. In addition to these course outlines, special curriculum materials have been written for citizenship and vocational ESL classes.

Teachers also receive sample lesson plans, including ones for multilevel instruction, and a list of SCANS (Secretary's Commission on Achieving Necessary Skills) competencies to integrate into their courses. Following a competency-based model, the course outlines are treated as menus from which teachers choose the competencies that relate to the learners' needs in their classrooms. Sample needs assessment forms are available to the teachers to use with their learners. Teachers are also encouraged to use a variety of instructional methods, according to learner needs. If a need arises in the classroom that is not listed on the course outline, a teacher has the freedom to diverge and teach to the targeted competency.

At the beginning of each year, the ESL resource office disseminates a list of recommended textbooks and materials for each level. Teachers may order class sets of books and materials that are appropriate. There is no mandated textbook. Each center has a resource library for ESL materials, and there is a district ESL library and resource center that contains materials for reference and check-out. Materials are approved that meet the criteria in the statewide instructional standards for ESL. A textbook committee reviews new materials to make sure that they meet these standards; they use a checklist that includes questions, such as the following: Are the materials culturally sensitive? Do they provide activities that address a variety of learning styles? Faculty staff development mini-grant funds also provide the opportunity for ESL faculty to develop curriculum materials that support the program.

Instruction

Instruction is designed to support the nine instructional standards identified in the statewide *Model Standards*. Teachers are trained to use approaches that meet the needs of their learners. The most common approach used is a competency-based approach in which language is taught in the context of key life skills that learners need in their roles as parents, workers, community members, and learners. For example, learners may be taught the language needed to express problems to a doctor. In a higher level class, in which learners are preparing for the TOEFL exam, however, learners may spend more time practicing test taking skills, writing essays, and correcting grammar errors, under a grammar-based approach. In a family literacy class, in a discussion of a community problem (e.g., housing rental rates being raised too frequently), the teacher may use a participatory approach and facilitate instruction to enable learners to solve the community problem (e.g., write letters to the apartment managers).

Rather than separate classes in listening, speaking, reading, and writing, the core classes integrate the teaching of listening, speaking, reading, and writing. For example, in a housing unit, learners may learn how to describe problems to an apartment manager over the telephone and in writing through a complaint letter. In a typical 3-hour class, learners will focus on developing their listening and speaking skills before the break and practice reading and writing after the break. Before presenting new material, the teacher facilitates an activity in which learners share what they already know about the topic from their experiences in their own country or in the United States. This helps the teacher target instruction to the levels of the learners. During the class period, it is recommended that at least 50 % of the time be devoted to interactive practice of the language patterns being learned. During this time the teacher is a facilitator helping learners complete communicative tasks. The program continues to encourage teachers to make their classes even more learner centered than teacher centered.

Teachers are also encouraged to manage their classrooms so that learners apply SCANS skills such as participating in teamwork, monitoring their own progress, and organizing their materials.

Where possible, the teacher uses authentic materials or real-life situations to demonstrate use of the language. For example, to practice taking a message over the telephone, learners may listen to real messages or actually take turns taking messages on the classroom telephone if there is one. Teachers use a variety of techniques to bring about more interaction in the classroom. Cooperative learning is used frequently, as is problem solving and role play. In many instances, teachers have used the problem solving technique to solve classroom problems related to cultural misunderstandings. Counselors at the main centers also conduct special group meetings to educate learners about cultural differences. Some teachers engage their learners in projects, such as creating a class newsletter or a recipe book. In many classes, teachers facilitate activities in which small groups make presentations to their classmates on their native countries and customs.

Most teachers do not have the training to facilitate project-based instruction. Generally, only the vocational ESL (VESL) labs have had the opportunity to integrate computer technology into instruction. In these classes, learners use different types of software to improve their skills and type their writing assignments on the computer before turning them in. Several classrooms now have Internet connections. The goal is to have at least one computer connected to the Internet in every ESL classroom at the main centers.

During instruction there is a very supportive, nonthreatening environment for language learning. The teacher does not call on individuals to perform until they have practiced language patterns in the whole group and small groups or pairs. The teacher uses a lot of visuals or other props to demonstrate meaning in a variety of ways. All of the beginning-level classes have realia to implement more kinesthetic learning tasks. In most multilevel classes, the teacher relies on grouping strategies to meet differing needs or gives out different materials to groups at different levels. There are few instructional assistants to help in multilevel classes. There are no native language literacy classes. Before standardized testing sessions, teachers use practice testing exercises to teach the basic skills of taking these tests, including the filling out of bubbles to complete answers on a scannable form.

Learner Recruitment, Intake, and Orientation

On a yearly basis, the program reviews community demographic studies to identify the population in need of English language instruction. Through outreach to community agencies, the program is kept informed of the arrival of new immigrant populations that need to be served. The school distributes flyers, some of them in other languages than English, to key institutions in the community, advertising its classes and programs. In front of key facilities housing English classes, there are colored banners advertising free English classes. In addition, the school places some ads in native language newspapers in the community but usually does not have the budget to do this on a regular basis. The ESL program also has a Web site that describes its program.

When learners come to enroll in English classes, they go through an assessment and orientation process in which they complete a learner profile form, take a short reading and writing test, and participate in an oral interview designed by the program. The results from this assessment determine the level of class into which the learner is placed. Scores on the oral interview test are correlated with the seven levels of instruction. At the time of placement, learners receive a letter welcoming them to the program, written in their native language. Matriculation counselors also give orientation presentations twice a year in the intermediate and advanced ESL classes advising learners about educational and vocational options after ESL. If classes are full, the learner is placed on a waiting list and notified when there is an opening. As desired, the learner may also be referred to additional special classes, such as pronunciation or writing. On a monthly basis, the program tallies the placement information in order to identify program trends and needs.

Learner Retention and Transition

The ESL program is operated on an open entry, open exit basis. Learners may enroll at any time during the semester and may exit or move to the next level when they are ready. Classes are scheduled at different times—morning, afternoon, and evening—to accommodate the needs of the learners. Some classes are 3 hours in duration; others are 2 hours. There are also some Friday evening and Saturday morning classes.

Several strategies are used to improve retention and transition. Twice a semester, the counselors visit classes to describe all aspects of the program and qualifications for entering job training classes or postsecondary educational institutions. Following these matriculation presentations, learners are urged to see the counselors for individual help. Speakers from the credit side of the community college program are invited to inform the noncredit learners about their programs, but this is not always done at all the centers. Special accommodations are provided for learners with disabilities. When learners are absent for an extended period of time, teachers send bilingual postcards to them to encourage them to return to classes; at some centers, the clerical staff call learners to document reasons for their absences.

The program does not provide childcare to learners attending the main centers. Through special funding, some babysitting is provided to learners attending special ESL family literacy classes at the elementary schools. The program does not provide transportation. There is no distance-learning program to accommodate learners who cannot attend during regular hours. The program also does not have sufficient funding to provide needed tutors or instructional assistants. The program also has not had the personnel to formally study and analyze retention patterns among the learner population.

Assessment and Learner Gains

The program has a process for assessing learners' skills upon entrance to the program, for assessing progress through the program, and for a system to document course completion. To identify learner needs and goals, learners complete a learner profile form upon entrance. As mentioned above, learners' linguistic levels are identified through a short reading and writing test and an oral interview test designed by the program.

To assess progress, teachers use a variety of strategies. There is no program-developed standardized test to monitor progress. Many teachers administer tests they have developed themselves. Some teachers have learners maintain portfolios of their work, which can be evaluated at the end of the semester. For each level, key competencies have been identified as criteria for level completion. Teachers have access to performance based measures to assess mastery of these key competencies. When learners satisfactorily demonstrate these key competencies, they are awarded certificates of completion for the level.

Because the state mandates standardized testing, the above performance-based system for documenting level completion is not required and only used on a voluntary basis by certain teachers. In the family literacy classes outcomes such as how frequently parents read to their children are documented over time, and gains in this area are also reported. Many classes also utilize checklists or learner self-assessment surveys to measure progress and achievement. In order to qualify for supplemental funding provided by the Adult Education and Literacy Act, the program administers CASAS (Comprehensive Adult Student Assessment System) standardized reading tests four times a year. For every significant gain on paired test scores, the program receives funding. Because these test score gains are tied to funding, this standardized testing is required in a majority of the classes. Test score results are shared with the teachers and learners, and instruction is targeted toward improving reading skills in the identified weak areas. The data from this testing are electronically stored via a software program in a data base and submitted to the state each year. As part of the pre- and post-CASAS testing, learner results in the area of goal attainment are tallied on a yearly basis to show positive outcomes and reported to the state. Individual test scores can be retrieved from the school's management information system. Because funding is tied to scores on the CASAS pre-/posttests, teachers are trained to administer the tests correctly and are encouraged to teach their learners how to take standardized tests. Overcrowding in many of the classrooms, however, is not conducive to appropriate test conditions, and the teachers often complain about this.

Other assessment tools used to advise learners of their progress toward meeting their goals include practice Test of English as a Foreign Language (TOEFL) tests and the Combined English Language Skills Assessment (CELSA) placement test used to place ESL learners into the credit community college program. According to the results of assessment, counselors advise learners about matriculation to other programs and schools.

Employment Conditions and Staffing

Being part of a community college system, there is an hourly hiring process and a contract hiring process for instructional and noninstructional staff. The contract hiring process is more formal. Approximately 30% of the ESL faculty have 10-month contracts; 70% are hired on an hourly basis. Both contract and hourly faculty must meet statewide minimum qualifications for teaching ESL, which include a bachelor's degree and evidence of formal ESL training, such as an ESL certificate or degree in TESOL. After meeting minimum qualifications, hourly candidates must teach a demonstration lesson in a beginning-level classroom to demonstrate their teaching skills. Each site also has some instructional assistants who assist with the placement of ESL learners, assessment, and instruction in the lower levels. These assistants are selected for their abilities to represent the various learner populations in the program.

The ESL program has an instructional leader (member of the ESL faculty) at each site who coordinates the ESL program. This instructional leader has a 100% contract and meets the minimum qualifications required of all ESL faculty, which include a bachelor's degree and evidence of formal ESL training, such as an ESL certificate or MA in TESOL. There is also a program-wide ESL coordinator who assists with program planning, curriculum development, scheduling of classes, the hiring of new teachers and aides, assessment procedures, and staff development to new and continuing teachers.

The teachers in the program belong to a union under the American Federation of Teachers. The union bargains for improved compensation and working conditions. Under the union agreement, all faculty and staff have access to a grievance procedure. Teachers with contracts have full benefits, including health insurance, life insurance, and dental insurance. Hourly teachers, representing the majority of the faculty do not receive these benefits. Both hourly and contract teachers are placed on salary scales that provide increased pay with each year of service and additional increments with a master's degree or a number of units above the master's degree. There is a category called *priority re-hire* for teachers who have been consistently employed for a certain number of years. Whereas hourly employees may be laid off at any time with no prior notice, priority rehire teachers must be offered alternative assignments over hourly teachers if their classes close due to insufficient enrollment. Before the start of a semester, all teachers are given their assignments in writing; however, hourly teachers are not guaranteed employment for the semester. All teachers receive a certain amount of sick leave per year. They also receive a specific number of personal leave days per year.

Teachers generally work in safe environments because of enforced building codes that relate to educational facilities in public education. Proper ventilation is sometimes a problem in the older buildings that become overcrowded due to large class size.

Professional Development and Staff Evaluation

Once hired, both hourly and contract teachers receive an orientation to the program and are encouraged to attend a series of workshops on practical techniques for teaching adult-level ESL. A few years ago, special training workshops were held for the administrators in the program on model standards for teaching ESL, but those have not been offered since then. There is a need for more consistent training on cross-cultural awareness and communication for the faculty and staff.

With supplementary state and federal funds, the ESL resource teacher and ESL site department chairs coordinate staff development activities throughout the year. A faculty needs assessment in the fall identifies the desired areas for staff development. These activities include workshops on special topics, book fairs by publishers, networking meetings, guest speakers on special topics, peer tutoring, and special curriculum projects. These funds also support teachers to attend local, state, and national conferences related to ESL. Teachers who present workshops at conferences are approved for more funding than those who are not presenting. The most popular conference attended is the statewide ESL conference. Teachers are not paid to attend staff development activities. Sometimes released time from the classroom is provided so that teachers can attend special training workshops on assessment. There is also a district ESL resource library from which teachers may check out texts and materials for use in their classes. The ESL Resource Office also publishes a newsletter three or four times a year, making teachers aware of new materials and ideas for teaching. Although the program encourages teachers to join professional ESL organizations like TESOL, it does not pay for memberships. At the end of each year, the ESL program has a luncheon to acknowledge teachers who have participated in professional development activities.

Official faculty evaluations are required for contract faculty and conducted on a regular basis, usually every 2–3 years. The evaluation process consists of an administrative evaluation and peer evaluation. An optional learner evaluation of the teacher is also possible. At the end of the evaluation process, if necessary, the teacher has the opportunity to develop a performance improvement plan.

Support Services

Being part of a large community college program, there are a variety of support services for the ESL program. Each site has counselors available to advise learners, including learning disability specialists to identify learners with special needs or need for special accommodations. Specific procedures exist for referring learners to these specialists. Although childcare is not offered for most of the ESL program, it is offered in a specially funded ESL program that provides ESL instruction to parents of elementary school aged children. The program maintains linkages with community agencies who provide other services, such as immigration counseling, health services, job counseling and placement, and family counseling. The ESL resource teachers also invite speakers to speak to the ESL learners periodically on special topics, such as home safety, environmental tobacco smoke, and family planning.

Self-Review Instrument Samples for Program 1

Curriculum and Instructional Materials

C. The curriculum includes goals, objectives, outcomes, approaches, methods, activities, materials, technological resources, and evaluation measures that are appropriate for meeting learners' needs and goals.

Measures

To score a 2 or 3, all the measures should be in place.

✓ 1 The curriculum addresses the needs and goals of learners identified through needs assessment activities.

✓ 2 The curriculum includes the following:

- ✓ goals
- ✓ objectives
- ✓ approaches
- ✓ methods
- ✓ activities
- ✓ materials
- ✓ technological resources
- ✓ expected outcomes
- ✓ evaluation measures
- __ other : ______________

___ Other: ________________________

Sample Evidence

✓ curricular document that includes
- ✓ course outline
- __ guidelines or framework
- __ record of emerging objectives

✓ results of learner needs assessments

__ other: ________________________

Comments

Technological resources (e.g., ESL Web sites and software appropriate for curriculum) are in the process of being added.

Action Plan/Next Steps

1. Integrate technological resources into curriculum guidelines.
2. Write curriculum materials to support the integration of technology into the ESL classroom (e.g., basic computer literacy lessons for beginning-level ESL learners).

Score

0	1	2	(3)	NA
Not in place			Well developed	

Priority

High Low

Professional Development

H. The program supports collaboration among adult ESL teachers, instructional personnel in other content areas, K–12 English and ESL teachers, support service providers, workplace personnel, and representatives of programs to which students transition.

Measures

To score a 2 or 3, the * measure should be in place.

*__1 The program supports the attendance of its faculty and staff at meetings to collaborate with other educational and community groups, such as
- __ community agencies: __________
- __ K–12 schools: __________
- __ educational oversight and policy groups (e.g., school board)
- __ workplace providers: __________
- __ other segments of own educational program (e.g., adult basic education [ABE] program, graduate equivalency diploma [GED]/high school program, vocational training programs): __________
- __ colleges: __________
- __ support service providers: __________
- __ outside job training programs
- __ business/industries

✓ 2 The program supports the joint use of facilities or resources.

✓ 3 The program provides technological resources and support for joint projects such as the following:
- __ transitioning projects
- __ collaborative learning
- __ research
- ✓ instructional projects

____ Other: __________

Action Plan/Next Steps

1. Seek funding for special grants to support teachers to collaborate with workplace providers, K–12 schools, ABE and GED programs, and credit ESL program.

Sample Evidence

✓ memorandum of understanding agreements between agencies
__ meeting notes/agendas
__ interviews with instructors
✓ grants that require collaboration
__ reports from collaborative projects
✓ other: joint use agreements for classroom space

Comments

The ESL resource teacher has release time to attend meetings to collaborate with other groups, but the teachers almost never are supported to attend meetings of this kind.

Score

0 (1) 2 3 NA

Priority

High Low

*Comment on scoring: This item received a score of 1 because the * measure was not checked, meaning that the item could not receive a score of 2 or 3. Although this institution has a resource instructor who attends meetings to collaborate with other educational and community groups, the majority of teachers are not supported to do this. There* *is little opportunity for instructors to meet with other instructors or representatives from other educational institutions or community groups.*

Summary Scores and Action Plan

Directions: Transfer your program's individual scores for each standard to this chart to analyze the strengths and areas for improvement for each part of your program. Record the proposed steps for improvement in the box titled "Action Plan" at the end of each section. Then, under "Priority Areas for Improvement," list the standards category and specific standards that are most in need of improvement, based on the results of this program review.

Scoring Key:

0—Program component not in place
1—Program component somewhat in place
2—Program component in place
3—Program component in place and well developed
NA—Not applicable to my program or not assessed at this time

1. Program Structure and Administration

Specific Standards	0	1	2	3	NA
A. Mission statement, philosophy, and goals				✓	
B. Administrative system				✓	
C. Sound financial management procedures				✓	
D. Accountability plan				✓	
E. Clear communication and linkages with internal and external stakeholders				✓	
F. Procedure for ensuring confidentiality				✓	
G. Equipment for daily operations and efficient record keeping				✓	
H. Appropriate facilities and resources for instruction				✓	
I. Courses of sufficient intensity and duration; flexible schedules; and convenient locations for learners				✓	
J. Learner-teacher ratio conducive to meeting learner needs and goals		✓			
K. (See Standard 2, Curriculum and Instructional Materials)					
L. (See Standard 3, Instruction)					
M. (See Standard 6, Assessment and Learner Gains)					
N. (See Standard 7, Employment Conditions and Staffing)					

Program Planning

Specific Standards	0	1	2	3	NA
O. Planning process		✓			
P. Technology plan	✓				
Q. Plan for outreach, marketing, and public relations		✓			
Overall Score for Standard Category			✓		

Action Plan

1. Develop a technology plan.
2. Improve the program planning and review process, eliciting more input from external stakeholders.
3. Improve marketing and outreach.
4. Develop policy for appropriate class size to meet learner needs.

2. Curriculum and Instructional Materials

Specific Standards	0	1	2	3	NA
A. Process for developing curriculum				✓	
B. Compatibility with principles of second language acquisition, mission, and philosophy of program				✓	
C. Goals, objectives, outcomes, approaches, methods, activities, materials, technological resources, and evaluation measures				✓	
D. Measurable learning objectives				✓	
E. Materials easily accessible, up to date, appropriate for adult learners, suitable for variety of learning styles, culturally sensitive, and oriented to needs of learners				✓	
F. Ongoing process for curriculum revision		✓			
Overall Score for Standard Category				✓	

Action Plan

1. Do curriculum review on a more regular basis; reinstate a textbook review committee.
2. Invite external stakeholders to provide input during curriculum review process.

3. Instruction

Specific Standards	0	1	2	3	NA
A. Activities adhere to adult learning principles and second language acquisition				✓	
B. Varied instructional approaches according to needs of learners			✓		

C. Learners take active role in learning process				✓	
D. Focus on acquisition of communication skills				✓	
E. Integration of four language skills				✓	
F. Varied activities according to different learning styles and special learning needs				✓	
G. Variety of grouping strategies and interactive tasks				✓	
H. Activities accommodate multilevel groups of learners, especially those with minimal literacy skills			✓		
I. Activities develop language for critical thinking, problem solving, team participation, and study skills			✓		
J. Use of authentic resources		✓			
K. Use of appropriate technologies		✓			
L. Integration of language and culture				✓	
M. Preparation of learners for formal and informal assessment			✓		
Overall Score for Standard Category			✓		

Action Plan

1. Increase integration of technology into classroom instruction.
2. Train teachers how to incorporate more technology.
3. Increase degree of learner centered instruction by providing more training and coaching for newer teachers.

4. Learner Recruitment, Intake, and Orientation

Specific Standards	0	1	2	3	NA
A. Effective procedures for identifying and recruiting adult ESL learners			✓		
B. Variety of recruitment strategies			✓		
C. Materials reach population in multiple languages as needed		✓			
D. Evaluation of effectiveness of recruitment strategies			✓		
E. Intake process, orientation to the program, and referral services as needed				✓	
Overall Score for Standard Category			✓		

Action Plan

1. Investigate ways to publicize program in more languages representative of learner population.

5. Learner Retention and Transition

Specific Standards	0	1	2	3	NA
A. Enrollment and attendance procedures that support demands on adult learners		✓			
B. Encouragement to reach goals		✓			
C. Accommodation of special needs of learners		✓			
D. Contact with learners with irregular attendance patterns/acknowledgment of good attendance		✓			
E. Appropriate support for transition to other programs		✓			
Overall Score for Standard Category		✓			

Action Plan

1. Develop a distance-education program.
2. Develop some on-line courses.
3. Develop methods to analyze retention patterns and identify strategies to improve retention.
4. Increase staffing to follow up on learners with irregular attendance patterns.

6. Assessment and Learner Gains

Assessment Policy

Specific Standards	0	1	2	3	NA
A. Assessment policy			✓		
B. Process of assessment for placement, progress, and exit from program			✓		
C. Ongoing and appropriately scheduled assessment			✓		
D. Procedures for collecting and reporting data on gains and outcomes			✓		
E. Appropriate facilities, equipment, supplies, and personnel for assessment			✓		
Types of Assessment					
F. Identification of learners' needs and goals			✓		
G. Assessment of language proficiency levels in listening, speaking, reading, and writing, including native language literacy and learning disabilities		✓			
H. Variety of assessments, including reliable and valid standardized assessment tools			✓		
Uses of Assessment					
I. Assessment information aids curriculum development			✓		
J. Assessment results shared with learners			✓		

K. Assessment documents learners' progress toward advancement to other programs		✓			
L. Results provide information about educational gains and outcomes			✓		
Learner Gains					
M. Process to identify short- and long-term goals and progress toward attainment of goals			✓		
N. Process to demonstrate skill-level improvements in listening, speaking, reading, and writing			✓		
O. Process to demonstrate progress in nonlinguistic areas		✓			
Overall Score for Standard Category			✓		

Action Plan

1. Develop program-based criteria and testing for level exit, particularly in listening and speaking skills.
2. Develop ways to document and report progress in nonlinguistic areas.
3. Develop tracking system to document advancement of learners to credit-bearing community college program or other programs.

7. Employment Conditions and Staffing

Specific Standards	0	1	2	3	NA
A. Appropriate compensation and benefits			✓		
B. Professional treatment of staff		✓			
C. Safe and clean working environment				✓	
D. Hiring of qualified teachers trained in ESL				✓	
E. Hiring of staff with appropriate training in cross-cultural communication			✓		
F. Trained support staff for effective program operation			✓		
Overall Score for Standard Category			✓		

Action Plan

1. Develop procedures to provide more advanced warning to teachers of class closures.
2. Work toward providing more 100% contracts to teachers.
3. Increase number of contract-classified staff to support program.

8. Professional Development and Staff Evaluation

Specific Standards	0	1	2	3	NA
A. Orientation for new ESL administrative, instructional, and support staff			✓		

B. Professional development plan, including resources to implement plan			✓		
C. Opportunities to expand knowledge of trends, technologies, research, and best practices				✓	
D. Opportunities for administrators/ evaluators to gain knowledge of effective strategies in adult-level ESL		✓			
E. Variety of professional development activities, including practice and follow-up			✓		
F. Training in assessment procedures and use of results				✓	
G. Encouragement to join professional ESL organizations		✓			
H. Support of collaboration of teachers with other programs		✓			
I. Recognition of participation in professional development activities				✓	

Staff Evaluation

Specific Standards	0	1	2	3	NA
J. Process for regular evaluation of staff			✓		
K. Anonymous evaluation of staff by learners			✓		
L. Opportunity to develop performance improvement plans			✓		
Overall Score for Standard Category			✓		

Action Plan

1. Develop ways to increase awareness among administrators and staff of ESL methodology and learner needs.
2. Improve teaching training for newer teachers and monitor application of new strategies after training.
3. Provide opportunities for teachers to collaborate more with other educational programs and the community.

9. Support Services

Specific Standards	0	1	2	3	NA
A. Access to a variety of services		✓			
B. Process for identifying learning disabilities			✓		
C. Linkages with cooperating agencies		✓			
Overall Score for Standard Category		✓			

Action Plan

1. Increase support services for learners (e.g., babysitting, counseling).
2. Improve linkages with community agencies to provide support services.

Priority Areas for Improvement

Standards Category	Specific Standards
Program Structure and Administration	O, P, Q
Learner Retention and Transition	D, E
Assessment	G, K, O
Support Services	A, C

Discussion of Scores for Program 1

Program 1 is a large, institution-based adult education program. As a result, most of the measures are scored as being "in place" (scored with a 2) or "in place and well developed" (scored with a 3). The areas needing improvement are scored with a 0 or 1. This program has only one 0 score signifying that a program component is "not in place." Program 1 has not written a technology plan yet, so that is a priority item for action, as indicated at the end of the Program Structure and Administration section of the Summary Scores and Action Plan Chart.

At the end of each section of the summary scoring chart, there is an opportunity to list proposed action plan items focused on measures that need improvement. For example, the action plan items under Program Structure and Administration are to develop a technology plan, improve the program planning and review process by getting more input from external stakeholders, improve marketing and outreach, and develop a policy for appropriate class size to meet learner needs.

In the area of Assessment and Learner Gains, Program 1's action plan items are to develop program-based criteria and testing for level exit, particularly in listening and speaking skills, develop ways to document and report progress in nonlinguistic skills, and develop a tracking system to document advancement of learners to other educational or vocational programs.

Many of the action plan items after each section relate to integrating more technology into instruction, such as distance-learning and on-line learning options. The results from Program 1's self-review process clearly indicate that integrating technology into instruction is an area for improvement.

At the end of the summary scoring chart under "Priority Areas for Improvement," each program may choose the most important standards to focus on and improve. For Program 1, four standards were chosen:

1. Program Structure and Administration
2. Learner Retention and Transition
3. Assessment and Learner Gains
4. Support Services

Program personnel could take the high priority items in these four areas and develop an action plan defining what steps might be taken to improve performance within the targeted standards and within what time frames. Although a program may list many action plan items under each section of standards, it may not be able to address them at the same time. Under Priority Areas for Improvement, program personnel have the opportunity to choose the most critical ones to address in light of program resources and funding constraints.

Program 2: Volunteer-Based Adult ESL Program

Narrative

Program Structure, Administration, and Planning

ESL Program 2 is part of a volunteer-based adult literacy organization that also offers limited amounts of basic reading and writing instruction to native speakers of English and, in special cases, offers GED preparation. The program serves approximately 650 ESL learners, with approximately 450 in small classes and the rest in one-to-one instruction. The organization in its current form is the result of a recent merger of local affiliates of both major national volunteer adult literacy organizations, and it maintains its affiliation with both. A volunteer board of directors oversees general operations and is active in fund-raising. Many board members are also active in coordination of instruction and serve as teachers and trainers. A paid executive director manages day-to-day operations and finances and also takes a leading role in publicity and fund-raising. There is also a paid program director who organizes training and coordinates tutor-learner matches. Both the executive director and the program director oversee data collection, prepare state reports, and coordinate the functioning of program-run centers. A program committee, made up of volunteers, is responsible for creating curriculum guidelines and selecting textbooks. The program committee chair also plays a role in coordinating tutor training.

The ESL program serves primarily low-income immigrants and refugees from diverse national and language backgrounds; learners range in age from 16 to 80. The program offers a limited number of advanced conversation groups, which meet at the local university and are attended mainly by university learners. The program focus, however, is adult English learners at the preliteracy/beginning through low intermediate levels, with approximately 50–60% at the literacy to beginning levels. Preliteracy learners receive one-to-one tutoring. The program tries to get all others into small-group classes. Instruction takes place at centers throughout the county, run by the program but housed in various host institutions, including libraries, a YMCA, community centers, apartment-complex club houses, and churches; approximately half of the centers are in local elementary schools. A volunteer center supervisor from the program is responsible for issues of access to rooms, basic upkeep, and availability of resource materials. Twenty centers provide one-to-one instruction, often with several tutor-learner pairs meeting concurrently in the same room. The other centers provide small-group class instruction. In the centers at elementary schools, learners are mostly parents of learners at a given school, but the classes there are not restricted to the parents. Enrollment is open-entry/open-exit. A few centers offer only specific levels of instruction; but most offer all levels (depending on demand/enrollment), with a lot of multi-level classes. Classes at the schools meet in available classrooms, cafeterias, or teachers' rooms. Tutors take along their own white boards, as well as any needed instruction materials; the program provides a number of traveling resource-book collections, brought to centers by either the center supervisor or a tutor.

Program headquarters are in a new building, donated and built for the program by a local service organization. The building contains offices for the directors, a library/resource center, a computer classroom, space for pre- and in-service training, a copy machine, and preparation space for tutor use. A newly formed learner support group meets at headquarters. Tutoring groups do not meet there.

Under Board leadership, the overall organization has begun a strategic planning process to build for future needs and ensure meeting state requirements. A recent grant provided money for computers and instructional software. One of the Board members has conducted an informal review of technology needs and the options available on the market, but information gathering about overall program needs has so far been more ad hoc than planned and organized to ensure that community needs are clearly met. Approximately half of program funding comes from state grants, recognizing that, in particular, the ESL program helps meet a critical need in the region for ESL instruction. The program's long-term goal, however, is to wean itself away from reliance on the state. Other funding comes from individual or corporate donations and grants from community or national service organizations. To meet reporting requirements of the state, the program has a system for tutors to submit attendance and contact hours in writing, but many tutors, who were used to merely calling in the hours worked, still resist complying with the written requirements. Trained, experienced tutors in particular resent the reporting system, feeling that the program doubts their performance.

The program maintains a core set of instructional offerings but attempts as much as possible to meet the needs of the community and the learners and to respond to requests for specific services. In the past, the program was very proactive in offering services to community agencies, but demand has grown over the years, and now, finding themselves spread as thin as they can be in terms of available tutors, the program addresses specific requests on a case-by-case basis. In some cases, individual tutors also bring recommendations based on opportunities or needs they see in the community; the program will address a proposal of this sort if resources are available. Although there is no formal plan for recruitment of tutors or learners, the program utilizes a variety of methods that have been effective over the years, including regular newspaper, TV, and radio announcements and tapping networks of referring organizations. Recruitment, publicity, and fund-raising are closely tied and often done through a single effort (e.g., a presentation at a community agency, corporation, or service organization).

Curriculum and Instructional Materials

The program has no required curriculum; it emphasizes teaching general language skills in the context of survival/life skills. Tutors are trained to teach all four language skills. The skill emphasis may vary depending on the needs and interests of a particular class, but generally aural/oral skills are identified as most needed and are most emphasized in instruction. There is a recommended core series of texts that use a communicative approach and life-skills content, but tutors are not required to use the series. Tutors select a text, with assistance from the program director, based on learner needs and, when identified, preferred learning styles. Tutors are trained to work with the goals elicited from learners at intake and to plan instruction to help meet those goals.

State requirements for funding focus on accomplishment of learner goals, but documenting that requires some use of formal, if not standardized, testing as well as more informal records, such as interviews and checklists. The program recognizes the need to better prepare tutors to maintain such records as well as to conduct needed testing. Because instruction focuses on learners' goals, tutors actively engage learners in planning instruction. The focus on oral skills and small-group (or individual) instruction means that learners are continually involved in the instructional activities. Tutors are encouraged to be flexible and willing to set aside a planned lesson if learners come with specific problems or issues that require attention and present urgent language needs.

Learner Recruitment, Intake, and Orientation

Learner recruitment is primarily (and successfully) done through word-of-mouth referrals. There are limited publicity efforts, mostly consisting of flyers posted at area agencies. Over the years, the program also has built up a referral network, including refugee agencies, parent liaisons at area schools, the Department of Probation, Vocational Rehabilitation offices, and the like. Referrals also come from the local community college, for learners who fall below the level of ESL instruction offered at the college as well as for learners who simply want more hours of instruction.

There is currently no formal orientation to the program. People who call the office are urged to come in individually to learn what services are available. In these cases, they often bring a friend or family member to translate. Many potential learners get information and an informal orientation to the program from the school-community liaison in the public schools. Learners are evaluated for placement when they begin attending a class or tutoring session. In classes, learners fill out a basic information form, based on a state form; this includes questions to elicit a learner's basic goals. The center supervisor collects these forms from the tutors and turns them in to the program director, who evaluates the responses to determine a learner's approximate level. Tutors working one-to-one use any of a variety of placement tools, primarily ones that are administered orally, including the ESLOA (English as a Second Language Oral Assessment), the John test, and the LitStart pretest. The program expects a new state placement tool to be available in the near future but also expects that it may be inappropriate for the very low levels of learners who come to the program.

Retention and Transition

With the goals lists elicited during intake and placement, tutors are able to monitor learners' progress toward their goals and encourage them to stick with their studies. The program does not have resources for regular follow-up with learners who miss classes, but many tutors take this on themselves. Although many classes have a core group of learners who stay for several years, it is not unusual to have learners who come for a short time and then stop; some of those learners may come back after a few years. A perceived program need is a system and the resources to document how many learners return, after how long a break, and to track, through exit interviews, why learners leave. The program office maintains information and contact lists so that learners can be referred for a wide variety of services. Referral is most often done by an individual tutor passing on the needed information. There is no formal follow-up on such referrals, only what might informally come out in later discussion between tutor and learner.

Key barriers to participation are child care and reliable transportation, private or especially public. The program does not provide child care. Title 1 schools, in which approximately half of the centers are located, do provide it and make it available to program participants for a small fee. At centers without child care (e.g., in churches or community centers), parents often bring their children to class, which can become quite disruptive. Learners working one-to-one with a tutor have to sign an agreement that they will find child care to ensure regular attendance at tutoring sessions.

Classes are scheduled at varying times of day to meet learner needs, and one-to-one tutoring times are established by tutor and learner negotiating a convenient time for both. The program is now getting requests for classes at night to accommodate people who work during the day. To date, the program has been unable to meet those requests due to problems finding available space, providing security, and finding tutors willing to teach at night. Although classes generally stop over the summer, at some of the school-based centers, the program provides an informal monthly conversation class over the summer to maintain connections with the learners. The ESL program, as noted, focuses primarily on lower levels of instruction. Learners who need advanced ESL or more specialized instruction (e.g., GED preparation) are referred to programs elsewhere in the county, particularly to the local community college. The program also tries, when a learner has reached an appropriate level of proficiency (or has been with the program for many years), to refer that learner to more level-appropriate classes elsewhere; such attempts are not always successful because learners often prefer the convenience and comfort of the less formal, volunteer-led setting.

Assessment and Learner Gains

Assessment is an area for which the program clearly recognizes the need for improvement—to meet program needs and provide documentation needed to meet state standards. The fluctuating attendance in classes creates a major challenge for doing regular assessment. In many classes, learners respond negatively to or are unfamiliar with formal assessments. The program is looking into establishing a system of portfolio assessment as more suitable for the learner population and will incorporate principles and techniques of portfolio assessment into tutor training. In general, the program is looking for more user-friendly ways to conduct ongoing assessment of learners.

Employment Conditions and Staffing

New tutors are recruited through a variety of publicity efforts: regular notices in the local newspaper, TV and radio public service announcements, bookmarks distributed at local libraries and bookstores, publicity generated around the achievements of an individual tutor, and public service events such as holiday gift-wrapping at a local bookstore. Board members and other volunteers include a recruiting pitch when fund-raising at local companies or speaking before other community groups, such as the Rotary Club. The program also gets referrals from the local volunteer center, and current tutors occasionally refer friends or relatives. Tutors only rarely come from the ethnic groups of the learner population; the program in particular tries to recruit from the local Hispanic population but has had very limited success in recruitment or retention from that group. Many of the tutors are retirees, but, increasingly, the program is getting younger and working volunteers.

Efforts are regularly made to encourage former learners to train as tutors, but most are reluctant to do so. Occasionally tutor volunteers come to the program to get experience before going into the Peace Corps. Quite a few of the tutors are winter visitors to the area; many of these have long-term learners with whom they work year after year. Only a few tutors drop out of the program right away; most continue for at least 1–2 years, and some have been tutoring for many years. The program encourages retention of tutors by trying as much as possible to focus on individuals' strengths in making tutoring/class assignments.

Professional Development and Evaluation

The program provides new tutors with a 12-hour preservice training workshop conducted over two weekends. This is required of all new tutors unless an individual can show that he or she is already certified in some way as an adult ESL teacher. Preservice ESL training primarily focuses on working with one recommended core series, using that as the framework for introducing and practicing general instructional techniques, as well as methods for adapting materials and developing non-text-based lessons to meet learners' needs and interests. In-service training workshops are conducted frequently on both specific techniques and more general instructional issues. The program asks (but cannot require) new tutors to come to at least the first in-service held after they start tutoring, to get updates, and to share initial experiences. There is informal follow-up with new tutors through calls from the program director or a center supervisor. For small-group classes, as much as possible, the program sets up team tutoring, often pairing a new volunteer with an experienced one. The program is also trying to set up a core group of mentors to work with new tutors, but this effort is still at an early stage of development.

Tutors are certified by both national organizations with which the program is affiliated. The training program is undergoing accreditation with one of those organizations; one of the ESL trainers is certified by the other. A challenge the program expects in the near future will be meeting requirements when the state establishes adult education certification. Tutors are encouraged to attend professional conferences; the program provides limited financial support for attending national conferences. The program also participates in meetings of a local literacy coalition and encourages tutors to attend and present at the local literacy mini-conference run by the coalition (and now conducted jointly with the local TESOL affiliate). Tutors are also encouraged to use ESL-focused Web sites as resources for ongoing professional development and instructional resources. Having computers at the program headquarters makes access to such Web sites possible, even for tutors without their own computers.

Because the teachers are volunteers, the program feels that a formal observation and evaluation program would be inappropriate. They feel, however, that learners let the program know about problems with tutors—by coming in to the main office to discuss problems with office staff or center supervisors, by requesting a change of class or tutor, or simply by dropping out (and then discussing the problem if there is a follow-up call from the program).

Self-Review Instrument Samples for Program 2

PROGRAM STRUCTURE AND ADMINISTRATION

I. The program provides courses of sufficient intensity and duration with flexible schedules to meet varied learner and community needs in convenient locations within the constraints of program resources.

Measures

To score a 2 or 3, all the measures should be in place.

✓ 1 Based on learner needs, the program offers one or more of the following:

- ✓ classes of different duration (e.g., 6 weeks, 12 weeks, 18 weeks)
- ✓ classes at different times (e.g., mornings, afternoons, evenings, weekends)
- ✓ classes at different locations (e.g., school, institution, church, mobile van, library, workplace)
- __ distance-learning options (e.g., check-out of videos, Internet-based classes, telecourses)

✓ 2 The program has a process to periodically review learner needs related to the scheduling of instruction (e.g., student surveys, community surveys, student focus groups).

___ Other: ____________________

Action Plan/Next Steps

Expand techniques used to review and gather information on learner and community needs related to scheduling (e.g., student focus groups).

Sample Evidence

__ survey results
✓ class schedules
✓ interviews with program staff
✓ flyers and advertisements showing course locations
✓ meeting minutes
✓ program reports
__ Web sites
__ needs assessments or surveys
__ focus group notes
__ distance-learning materials
✓ other: Interviews with learners and community contacts

Comments

Score

0 1 2 (3) NA

Priority

High Low

Assessment and Learner Gains

Assessment Policy

A. The program has a comprehensive assessment policy.

Measures

To score a 2 or 3, all the measures should be in place.

The policy has the following attributes:

___1 reflects the mission and goals of the program

___2 accommodates legal requirements

___3 reflects the needs of the learners and other stakeholders

___4 is linked to instructional objectives and activities

___5 is developed with input from internal and external stakeholders

___6 is based on principles of adult learning, second language acquisition, language learning pedagogy, literacy development for adults, and sound language testing principles and procedures

___ Other: ______________________

Action Plan/Next Steps

Develop an explicit assessment policy as part of current strategic planning process.

Sample Evidence

__ program guidelines
__ course outlines
__ grant guidelines
__ state funding guidelines or policies
__ teacher training materials
✓ interviews with program staff
__ accreditation self-study
__ program audit reports
__ other: ______________________

Comments

There is no formal assessment policy, and tutors are often resistant to using assessments.

Score

(0) 1 2 3 NA

Priority

High Low

B. The program has a process for assessing learners' skills and goals for placement into the program, documentation of progress within the program, and exit from the program. This includes appropriate assessment of learners with special learning needs.

Measures

To score a 2 or 3, all the * measures should be in place.

The program has a process for the following:

*✓1 assessing learners' needs and goals for placement into the program

*__2 documenting progress within the program

*__3 documenting criteria for exit from the program

__4 assessing learners with special needs

Sample Evidence

__ guidelines for testing
✓ sample assessments or tests
✓ interviews with staff
__ assessment reports
__ other: ____________________

Comments

Tutors are trained in goal-identification, and placement is done by using one of a variety of skills assessments but little assessment at other stages or for other purposes is done.

Action Plan/Next Steps

1. Identify effective skills assessment tools that meet needs and capabilities of program at all stages of learning.
2. Identify assessment needs for meeting funding requirements.

Score

0 (1) 2 3 NA

Priority

High Low

Summary Scores and Action Plan

Directions: Transfer your program's individual scores for each standard to this chart to analyze the strengths and areas for improvement for each part of your program. Record the proposed steps for improvement in the box titled "Action Plan" at the end of each section. Then under "Priority Areas for Improvement," list the standards category and specific standards that are most in need of improvement, based on the results of this program review.

Scoring Key:

0—Program component not in place
1—Program component somewhat in place
2—Program component in place
3—Program component in place and well developed
NA—Not applicable to my program or not assessed at this time

1. Program Structure and Administration

Specific Standards	0	1	2	3	NA
A. Mission statement, philosophy, and goals			✓		
B. Administrative system				✓	
C. Sound financial management procedures			✓		
D. Accountability plan		✓			
E. Clear communication and linkages with internal and external stakeholdersand external stakeholders			✓		
F. Procedure for ensuring confidentiality				✓	
G. Equipment for daily operations and efficient record keeping				✓	
H. Appropriate facilities and resources for instruction			✓		
I. Courses of sufficient intensity and duration; flexible schedules; and convenient locations for learners				✓	
J. Learner-teacher ratio conducive to learner needs and goals		✓			
K. (See Standard 2, Curriculum and Instructional Materials)					
L. (See Standard 3, Instruction)					
M. (See Standard 6, Assessment and Learner Gains)					
N. (See Standard 7, Employment Conditions and Staffing)					

Program Planning

Specific Standards	0	1	2	3	NA
O. Planning process		✓			
P. Technology plan			✓		

Q. Plan for outreach, marketing, and public relations			✓		
Overall Score for Standard Category			✓		

Action Plan

1. Develop process for soliciting input from learners; solicit from broader base of external stakeholders.
2. Improve reporting system.
3. Distribute program newsletter on regular basis to internal and external stakeholders.
4. Review retention records; analyze patterns relative to class size.
5. Ensure input from broad base of stakeholders in planning process; plan for ongoing program review.
6. Evaluate outreach efforts and results; create a more formal plan.

2. Curriculum and Instructional Materials

Specific Standards	0	1	2	3	NA
A. Process for developing curriculum		✓			
B. Compatibility with principles of second language acquisition, mission, and philosophy of program			✓		
C. Goals, objectives, outcomes, approaches, methods, activities, materials, technological resources, and evaluation measures		✓			
D. Measurable learning objectives		✓			
E. Materials easily accessible, up to date, appropriate for adult learners, suitable for variety of learning styles, culturally sensitive, and oriented to needs of learners					✓
F. Ongoing process for curriculum revision		✓			
Overall Score for Standard Category		✓			

Action Plan

1. Conduct organized needs assessment and formal curriculum review; plan for regularly scheduled review.
2. Expand curriculum to make explicit expected outcomes, learning objectives, technological resources.

3. Instruction

Specific Standards	0	1	2	3	NA
A. Activities adhere to adult learning principles and second language acquisition				✓	
B. Varied instructional approaches according to needs			✓		
C. Learners take active role in learning process			✓		
D. Focus on acquisition of communication skills				✓	

E. Integration of four language skills			✓		
F. Varied activities according to different learning styles and special learning needs			✓		
G. Variety of grouping strategies and interactive tasks				✓	
H. Activities accommodate multilevel groups of students, especially those with minimal literacy skills				✓	
I. Activities develop language for critical thinking, problem solving, team participation, and study skills			✓		
J. Use of authentic resources			✓		
K. Use of appropriate technologies			✓		
L. Integration of language and culture				✓	
M. Preparation of learners for formal and informal assessment		✓			
Overall Score for Standard Category			✓		

Action Plan

1. Provide in-service training to help instructors work with greater variety of approaches, techniques.
2. Help instructors build in more reading and writing activities, as appropriate to learners' needs, and more activities in which learners use resources outside of class.
3. Build in greater opportunities for use of varied technologies.

4. Learner Recruitment, Intake, and Orientation

Specific Standard	0	1	2	3	NA
A. Effective procedures for identifying and recruiting adult ESL learners				✓	
B. Variety of recruitment strategies				✓	
C. Materials reach population in multiple languages as needed		✓			
D. Evaluation of effectiveness of recruitment strategies			✓		
E. Intake process, orientation to the program, and referral services as needed		✓			
Overall Score for Standard Category			✓		

Action Plan

1. Make recruitment and intake materials available in native languages of potential learners and in forms suitable for persons with special needs.
2. Improve tracking of results of recruitment efforts and review for needed adjustments.
3. Implement an orientation process, including presentation in learners' native languages.

5. Learner Retention and Transition

Specific Standards	0	1	2	3	NA
A. Enrollment and attendance procedures that support demands on adult learners		✓			
B. Encouragement to reach goals		✓			
C. Accommodation of special needs of learners		✓			
D. Contact with learners with irregular attendance patterns/acknowledgment of good attendance		✓			
E. Appropriate support for transition to other programs		✓			
Overall Score for Standards Category		✓			

Action Plan

1. Implement orientation as noted above.
2. Expand ability of program to accommodate learners with special needs.

6. Assessment and Learner Gains

Assessment Policy

Specific Standards	0	1	2	3	NA
A. Assessment policy	✓				
B. Process of assessment for placement, progress, and exit from program		✓			
C. Ongoing and appropriately scheduled assessment		✓			
D. Procedures for collecting and reporting data on gains and outcomes		✓			
E. Appropriate facilities, equipment, supplies, and personnel for assessment		✓			
Types of Assessment					
F. Identification of learners' needs and goals		✓			
G. Assessment of language proficiency levels in listening, speaking, reading, and writing, including native language literacy and learning disabilities			✓		
H. Variety of assessments, including reliable and valid standardized assessment tools		✓			
Uses of Assessment					
I. Assessment information aids curriculum development		✓			
J. Assessment results shared with learners			✓		

K. Assessment documents learners' progress toward advancement to other programs		✓			
L. Results provide information about educational gains and outcomes		✓			
Learner Gains					
M. Process to identify short- and long-term goals and progress toward attainment of goals		✓			
N. Process to demonstrate skill-level improvements in listening, speaking, reading, and writing		✓			
O. Process to demonstrate progress in nonlinguistic areas			✓		
Overall Score for Standard Category		✓			

Action Plan

1. Identify assessment needs for meeting funding requirements; orient all program staff to requirements, importance of assessment to program, options and approaches to assessment.
2. Train instructional staff in assessment methods and materials suitable for learner population; follow up to ensure effective implementation.
3. Develop or adopt a more formal system of data collection; report and interpret results to program staff.
4. Integrate results of assessment into curriculum review and development process.

7. Employment Conditions and Staffing

Specific Standards	0	1	2	3	NA
A. Appropriate compensation and benefits					✓
B. Professional treatment of staff			✓		
C. Safe and clean working environment			✓		
D. Hiring of qualified instructors trained in ESL				✓	
E. Hiring of staff with appropriate training in cross-cultural communication		✓			
F. Trained support staff for effective program operation			✓		
Overall Score for Standard Category			✓		

Action Plan

1. Review and update program policies and procedures.
2. Create opportunities for support staff to expand cross-cultural training and experiences.

8. Professional Development and Staff Evaluation

Specific Standards	0	1	2	3	NA
A. Orientation for new ESL administrative, instructional, and support staff			✓		
B. Professional development plan including resources to implement plan		✓			
C. Opportunities to expand knowledge of trends, technologies, research, and best practices			✓		
D. Opportunities for administrators/ evaluators to gain knowledge of effective strategies in adult-level ESL		✓			
E. Variety of professional development activities, including practice and follow-up			✓		
F. Training in assessment procedures and use of results		✓			
G. Encouragement to join professional ESL organizations			✓		
H. Support of collaboration of instructors with other programs			✓		
I. Recognition of participation in professional development activities			✓		

Staff Evaluation

Specific Standards	0	1	2	3	NA
J. Process for regular evaluation of staff		✓			
K. Anonymous evaluation of staff by learners			✓		
L. Opportunity to develop performance improvement plans		✓			
Overall Score for Standard Category			✓		

Action Plan

1. Within overall program planning process, develop plan for ongoing staff development, including needed resources and budget, ongoing expansion of resource library, and links to community resources for training and professional development.
2. Within overall program planning process, develop a process for regular evaluation of staff, within constraints of program structure.

9. Support Services

Specific Standards	0	1	2	3	NA
A. Access to a variety of services			✓		
B. Process for identifying learning disabilities		✓			
C. Linkages with cooperating agencies			✓		
Overall Score for Standard Category			✓		

Action Plan

1. Update list of community services, particularly resources in learners' native languages.
2. Provide training and information on learning disabilities and identification in ESL learners.

Priority Areas for Improvement

Standards Category	Specific Standards
Program Structure and Administration	A, B—increase input from learners
Curriculum and Instructional Materials	A, C, D, F
Assessment and Learner Gains	all

Discussion of Scores for Program 2

Program 2 is part of a volunteer-based adult literacy organization. The organization's philosophy and structure influence the way that Program 2 deals with some areas of standards. In some sections, most or all of the measures are scored as being "in place" (scored with a 2) and in some cases as being "in place and well developed" (scored with a 3). In other sections, however, most of the measures are only "somewhat in place" (scored with a 1). These indicate areas the program needs to work on. For example, because there is no programwide assessment policy and only limited or idiosyncratic use of assessments, most items here receive a score of 2. This area of assessment is therefore one of the priority items for action. The program does, however, have at least some degree of virtually all measures, indicated by the fact that only one measure was marked as "not in place" (scored with a 0). Only one standard is scored as "NA," or not applicable to the program, and that is the standard for appropriate compensation and benefits for instructional staff, clearly not applicable to a volunteer program.

At the end of each section on the summary scoring chart there is an opportunity to list proposed action plan items focused on measures that need improvement. For example, the action plan items under Curriculum and Instruction are to conduct an organized needs assessment and formal curriculum review, with plans for regularly scheduled review, and to expand the curriculum in order to make explicit the expected outcomes, learning objectives, and technological resources available.

In the area of Assessment and Learner Gains, Program 2's action plan items are to identify assessment needs in order to meet funding requirements; orient all program staff (particularly volunteer instructors) to those requirements, to the importance of assessment to the program, and to options available for assessment; train staff in assessment methods and materials; develop or adopt a more formal system of data collection; and integrate the results of assessment into the curriculum review and development process.

Many of the action plan items after each section relate to improving data collection, formalizing processes and procedures that are done now on a relatively idiosyncratic basis, and creating opportunities for greater learner input and participation. The results from Program 2's self-review process indicate a need for greater input from learners and greater formalization of curriculum development and assessment.

At the end of the summary scoring chart, under "Priority Areas for Improvement," each program may choose the standards that it feels are most important to focus on. Program 2 chose three standards:

1. Program Structure and Administration
2. Curriculum and Instructional Materials
3. Assessment and Learner Gains

Program Structure and Administration is a section in which the program did generally well, scoring mainly 2s and 3s. But the program still felt the importance of increasing student input to the mission statement and goals of the program and to the administrative system. For Assessment and Learner Gains, the program felt that all standards in the section were important because there is so little that is done on an organized basis.

Program personnel could take the high-priority items in the three areas selected and develop an action plan defining what steps might be taken to improve performance with the targeted standards and within what time frames. Although a program might identify many action plan items under each standard, it may not be able to address all of them at the same time. Using the "Priority Areas for Improvement," program personnel have the opportunity to choose the most critical ones to address in light of program resources and funding constraints.

Part 4

Program Self-Review Instrument

1. Program Structure, Administration, and Planning

Program Structure and Administration

A. The program has a mission statement, a clearly articulated philosophy, and goals developed with input from internal and external stakeholders.

Measures

To score a 2 or 3, all of the measures should be in place.

___1 Input is solicited from internal stakeholders, which may include one or more of the following:

- __ administrators
- __ instructional staff
- __ support staff
- __ program volunteers
- __ learners
- __ other: ________________

___2 Input is solicited from external stakeholders, which may include one or more of the following:

- __ boards or advisory groups
- __ community and agency leaders
- __ business leaders
- __ employment and training agencies
- __ other educational or service providers
- __ federal, state, or local legislators
- __ funders
- __ other: ______________________

___3 A written mission statement is accessible.

___4 A clearly articulated philosophy exists.

___5 Program goals are identified.

___ Other: ______________________

Action Plan/Next Steps

Sample Evidence

- __ annual report
- __ mission statement
- __ accreditation report
- __ program publicity
- __ minutes from meetings with internal stakeholders
- __ minutes from meetings with external stakeholders
- __ other: ____________________

Comments

Score

0 1 2 3 NA

Priority

High Low

1. Program Structure, Administration, and Planning

Program Structure and Administration

B. The program has an administrative system (e.g., board of directors or advisory group and bylaws) that ensures participation of internal stakeholders, accountability, and effective administration of all program activities. (The system will vary according to whether the program is autonomous or affiliated with a larger institution or organization.)

Measures

To score a 2 or 3, the following measure should be in place.

____ The following internal stakeholders participate in the administrative system of the organization:

__ administrators
__ instructional staff
__ support staff
__ program volunteers
__ learners
__ other: ________________

Sample Evidence

__ written bylaws
__ flow chart of organization
__ list of board members or advisory group
__ accreditation report
__ shared governance guidelines
__ minutes from shared governance meetings
__ minutes from board or advisory group meetings
__ other: __________________

Comments

Action Plan/Next Steps

Score

0 1 2 3 NA

Priority

High Low

1. Program Structure, Administration, and Planning

Program Structure and Administration

C. The program has sound financial management procedures to collect and maintain fiscal information, guide program budgeting, ensure continuity of funding, and meet reporting requirements.

Measures

To score a 2 or 3, all of the measures should be in place.

___1 The program has an annual budget and a system for tracking expenditures within the budget.

___2 The program has a process for budget development that includes input from internal stakeholders, as appropriate.

___3 The program has procedures by which internal and external stakeholders are made aware of financial issues related to the program.

___4 The program has a process for reporting financial information as requested by funders.

___5 The program manages its finances in a manner that ensures continued funding within funding parameters.

___ Other: ____________________

Sample Evidence

__ program audit reports
__ financial reports
__ annual budget
__ interviews with program staff/business office
__ written policies

Comments

Action Plan/Next Steps

Score

0 1 2 3 NA

Priority

High Low

1. Program Structure, Administration, and Planning

Program Structure and Administration

D. The program has an accountability plan with a system for record keeping and reporting that is consistent with program policies and legal and funding requirements.

Measures

To score a 2 or 3, all the measures should be in place.

___1 The program demonstrates accountability by doing one or more of the following:

- __ meeting requirements during an audit procedure
- __ maintaining a record-keeping system that enables the program to report data requested by funders or educational agencies

___2 The program uses an up-to-date record-keeping and reporting system that supports program requirements.

___ Other: ____________________

Sample Evidence

- __ accountability plan
- __ program records
- __ policy manual
- __ grant guidelines
- __ state or local funding guidelines
- __ reports submitted to state

Comments

Action Plan/Next Steps

Score

0 1 2 3 NA

Priority

High Low

1. Program Structure, Administration, and Planning

Program Structure and Administration

E. The program fosters and maintains linkages and clear communication with internal and external stakeholders.

Measures

To score a 2 or 3, all of the measures should be in place.

___1 The program maintains linkages with one or more of the following external stakeholders:

- __ board or advisory group members
- __ community leaders
- __ business leaders
- __ employment or training agency personnel
- __ other educational or service provider
- __ federal, state, or local legislator
- __ member of other funding agency
- __ other: ________________

___2 The program maintains clear communication with all internal stakeholders (e.g., administrators, instructional staff, support staff, program volunteers, and learners).

___3 The program maintains good communication with its internal and external stakeholders by doing one or more of the following:

- __ meeting regularly with stakeholders
- __ publishing a program newsletter that is distributed to stakeholders
- __ sending regular memos to update stakeholders on program issues and events
- __ other: ________________

Action Plan/Next Steps

Sample Evidence

- __ memoranda of understanding
- __ minutes from meetings with stakeholders
- __ grant guidelines
- __ publicity and schedules or agendas from joint conferences and other programs
- __ newsletters
- __ press releases
- __ Web site

Comments

Score

0 1 2 3 NA

Priority

High Low

1. Program Structure, Administration, and Planning

Program Administration

F. The program has a procedure for ensuring confidentiality in communication with internal and external stakeholders.

Measures

To score a 2 or 3, all the * measures should be in place:

*___1 The program abides by the legal requirements regarding confidentiality, privacy, and release of public information.

___2 Students must sign waivers to release personal information (e.g., social security numbers).

*___3 Students' personal information is not displayed publicly without written permission.

*___4 Students' work is not published or disseminated without written permission.

*___5 Information about students is released to visitors to the program only with student permission within legal limitations.

Sample Evidence

__ written policy or rules
__ waiver forms for release of student personal information
__ education code regulations
__ other________________________

Comments

Action Plan/Next Steps

Score

0 1 2 3 NA

Priority

High Low

1. Program Structure, Administration, and Planning

Program Administration

G. The program provides equipment for daily operations and efficient record keeping.

Measures

To score a 2 or 3, all the measures should be in place.

___1 The program provides basic equipment for daily operations and efficient record keeping, which may include any of the following:

- __ computer-based management information system
- __ office space for managing records
- __ filing cabinets and drawers
- __ telephone system
- __ copiers

___2 Office supplies are available to support daily operations.

___ Other: ____________________

Sample Evidence

- __ inventory of equipment and supplies
- __ observation of daily operations
- __ interviews with program staff
- __ other: ______________________

Comments

Action Plan/Next Steps

Score

0 1 2 3 NA

Priority

High Low

1. Program Structure, Administration, and Planning

Program Structure

H. The program uses facilities and resources appropriate for adult ESL instruction, meeting the needs of learners and instructional staff. If a program is part of a larger institution, facilities meet standards equivalent to those of other programs.

Measures

To score a 2 or 3, all the measures should be in place.

___1 The program provides appropriate facilities for instruction, which include the following:
- __ well-ventilated classroom or learning space
- __ sufficient lighting
- __ adult-size tables and chairs
- __ access to clean restrooms
- __ handicapped accessibility
- __ emergency exits and instructions
- __ adequate storage for instructional materials and learner records

___2 Instructional areas receive regular custodial maintenance.

___3 The program provides appropriate equipment and supplies for instruction, which may include the following:
- __ whiteboard or blackboard
- __ flip chart
- __ overhead projector or document camera
- __ computer projector
- __ tape or CD player
- __ bulletin board space

___4 The program provides appropriate space for meeting individually with students.

___5 The program provides instructional staff with the following to support planning for instruction:
- __ an area to prepare for instruction (e.g., workroom, table space)
- __ supplies for preparation (e.g., scissors, paper, hole punch, transparencies, transparency markers)
- __ equipment for preparation (e.g., photocopier, computers, paper cutter, overhead projector, audiotape player)

___ Other: ________________

Action Plan/Next Steps

Sample Evidence

__ observation of facilities
__ interviews with learners
__ interviews with instructional staff
__ regular inspection reports on facilities
__ site/facility map or diagram

Comments

Score

0 1 2 3 NA

Priority

High Low

1. Program Structure, Administration, and Planning

Program Structure

I. The program provides courses of sufficient intensity and duration with flexible schedules to meet varied learner and community needs in convenient locations within the constraints of program resources.

Measures

To score a 2 or 3, all the measures should be in place.

___1 Based on learner needs, the program offers one or more of the following:

- __ classes of different duration (e.g., 6 weeks, 12 weeks, 18 weeks)
- __ classes at different times (e.g., mornings, afternoons, evenings, weekends)
- __ classes at different locations (e.g., school, institution, church, mobile van, library, workplace)
- __ distance-learning options (e.g., check-out of videos, Internet-based classes, telecourses)

___2 The program has a process to periodically review learner needs related to the scheduling of instruction (e.g., student surveys, community surveys, student focus groups).

____ Other: ______________________

Sample Evidence

__ survey results
__ class schedules
__ interviews with program staff
__ flyers and advertisements showing course locations
__ meeting minutes
__ program reports
__ Web sites
__ needs assessments or surveys
__ focus group notes
__ distance-learning materials
__ other: ______________________

Comments

Action Plan/Next Steps

Score

0 1 2 3 NA

Priority

High Low

1. Program Structure, Administration, and Planning

Program Administration

J. The program maintains a learner-teacher ratio conducive to meeting learning needs and goals.

Measures

To score a 2 or 3, all the measures should be in place.

___1 The program takes into consideration the following factors in determining the learner-teacher ratio:

- __ level of first language literacy
- __ learning disabilities in learners
- __ cultural backgrounds of learners
- __ space for instruction
- __ English proficiency level of students
- __ modes of instruction (e.g., computer lab vs. classroom with no computers)
- __ requirements of funders
- __ other: ________________

___2 The program analyzes the relationship between class size, attendance patterns, and learner retention.

___3 The program reviews research findings on class size and learning.

___4 The program recruits classroom aides, paraprofessionals, or volunteers to improve the learner-teacher ratio as needed.

___ Other: ____________________

Action Plan/Next Steps

Sample Evidence

- __ average class size data
- __ learner-teacher ratio data
- __ studies/reports of program trends in learner progress and class size
- __ interviews with learners
- __ learner surveys
- __ interviews with instructors
- __ learner retention data
- __ staffing chart showing numbers of paid instructors, paid classroom aides, paid paraprofessionals, volunteers, etc.
- __ other: ____________________

Our average class size is _________.

Our average learner-teacher ratio is _________.

Comments

Score

0 1 2 3 NA

Priority

High Low

Note: Self-review items for Standard K are in the Standards for Curriculum and Instructional Materials; for Standard L in Standards for Instruction; for Standard M in Standards for Assessment and Learner Gains; for Standard N in Standards for Employment Conditions and Staffing.

1. Program Structure, Administration, and Planning

Program Planning

O. The program has a planning process for initial program development and ongoing program improvement that is guided by evaluation and based on a written plan that considers targeted community demographics, retention patterns, learner needs, resources, local economic trends, and educational and technological trends in the field.

Measures

To score 2 or 3, all the measures should be in place.

The planning process includes all of the following:

___1 The process includes input from internal and external stakeholders.

___2 Program planning and review considers the following:

- __ community demographics
- __ learner retention patterns
- __ learner needs
- __ program resources
- __ local economic trends
- __ educational trends
- __ technological trends in the field

___3 The program review process is regularly scheduled to identify needs for program improvement.

___ Other: ____________________

Sample Evidence

- __ schedule of program review meetings
- __ program review documents
- __ program review schedule
- __ program review meeting notes or minutes
- __ interviews with program staff

Comments

Action Plan/Next Steps

Score

0 1 2 3 NA

Priority

High Low

1. Program Structure, Administration, and Planning

Program Planning

P. The program has a technology plan that is aligned with program goals and learner needs. The plan addresses the use, acquisition, and maintenance of technological resources and the training of program personnel.

Measures

To score 2 or 3, all the measures should be in place.

___1 The program conducts research to identify how technology can enhance teaching and learning in ESL.

___2 The program conducts needs assessments among learners and staff to determine the needs of learners related to technology.

___3 The technology plan addresses the following:

- __ learner needs
- __ what technology will be acquired and used
- __ how technology will be used
- __ methods and proposed budgets for acquiring technology (e.g., grants)
- __ how technology will be maintained
- __ what support is required to maintain technology and help users
- __ schedule for technology training for staff

___4 The program conducts a regular review of the technology plan.

___ Other: ____________________

Action Plan/Next Steps

Sample Evidence

- __ technology plan
- __ teacher training materials
- __ written guidelines for use of technology
- __ interviews with technology support staff
- __ needs assessment results
- __ learner interviews or surveys
- __ other: _____________

Comments

Score

0 1 2 3 NA

Priority

High Low

1. Program Structure, Administration, and Planning

Program Planning

Q. The program has a plan for outreach, marketing, and public relations to foster awareness and understanding of the program.

Measures

To score 2 or 3, all the measures should be in place.

___1 The plan is developed with input from internal and external stakeholders.

___2 The plan includes the following:

- __ identification of target audiences (e.g., learners, funders, partners, teachers, local community members, politicians)
- __ strategies for outreach, marketing, and public relations
- __ budget to support activities
- __ staffing needed to support the activities
- __ process for evaluating the results of outreach and marketing activities

___3 The program has a process for regular review of the plan.

___ Other: ____________________

Sample Evidence

__ outreach and marketing plan
__ program publicity
__ meeting minutes or notes
__ interviews with program staff
__ other: ____________________

Comments

Action Plan/Next Steps

Score

0 1 2 3 NA

Priority

High Low

2. Curriculum and Instructional Materials

A. The program has a process for developing curriculum that is based on a needs assessment of learners and includes participation and input from other stakeholders.

Measures

To score a 2 or 3, all the measures should be in place.

___1 The following are consulted in the development of the curriculum, as appropriate:

__ learners
__ instructors
__ administrators
__ content experts (e.g., adult learning specialists, ESL specialists, linguists, technology consultants, special learning needs specialists, counselors)
__ stakeholders in the community:
__social service agencies
__employers
__ethnic/cultural organizations
__businesses
__other educational institutions
__other:______________

___2 The needs assessment identifies learners' needs and goals in their roles as family members, community participants, workers, and lifelong learners.

____ Other: ____________________

Sample Evidence

__ minutes of curriculum meetings
__ learner needs assessment
__ instructor surveys or questionnaires
__ telephone notes
__ lists of participants or contributors
__ memos
__ agendas
__ written reviews of curriculum drafts
__ other: ________________________

Comments

Action Plan/Next Steps

Score

0 1 2 3 NA

Priority

High Low

2. Curriculum and Instructional Materials

B. The curriculum reflects the mission and philosophy of the program and is compatible with principles of second language acquisition for adult learners.

Measures

To score a 2 or 3, all the * measures should be in place.

*__1 The curriculum is relevant to adult learners (i.e., based on learners' interests, experience, and needs).

__2 The curriculum is cyclical (i.e., objectives are recycled in a variety of levels and contexts. For example, a beginning ESL course outline and intermediate ESL course outline include objectives on a similar topic, such as health, but the objectives on the intermediate outline address higher level language competencies).

*__3 The curriculum is compatible with the program's mission statement and philosophy (see Standard 1, A).

*__4 The curriculum is compatible with second language acquisition principles.

__ Other:____________________

Sample Evidence

__ Curricular document, such as
- __ course outline
- __ guidelines or framework
- __ record of emerging objectives

Comments

Action Plan/Next Steps

Score

0 1 2 3 NA

Priority

High Low

2. Curriculum and Instructional Materials

C. The curriculum includes goals, objectives, outcomes, approaches, methods, activities, materials, technological resources, and evaluation measures that are appropriate for meeting learners' needs and goals.

Measures

To score a 2 or 3, all the measures should be in place.

___1 The curriculum addresses the needs and goals of learners identified through needs assessment activities.

___2 The curriculum includes the following:

__ goals
__ objectives
__ approaches
__ methods
__ activities
__ materials
__ technological resources
__ expected outcomes
__ evaluation measures
__ other: _______________

___ Other: ___________________________

Sample Evidence

__ curricular document that includes
__ course outline
__ guidelines or framework
__ record of emerging objectives
__ results of learner needs assessments
__ other: ________________________

Comments

Action Plan/Next Steps

Score

0 1 2 3 NA

Priority

High Low

2. Curriculum and Instructional Materials

D. The curriculum specifies measurable learning objectives for each instructional offering for learners and is appropriate for learners in multilevel classes.

Measures

To score a 2 or 3, all the * measures should be in place.

*__1 Learning objectives are recorded.

*__2 Learning objectives describe measurable performance outcomes that can be assessed for documentation of progress or attainment (e.g., learners will be able to make a doctor's appointment; learners will be able to describe events in the past).

__3 Learning objectives accommodate learners at a variety of levels (e.g., a cross-listing of objectives at different levels within a topic area appears in the curriculum document).

____ Other:______________________

Sample Evidence

__ curriculum guide that includes learning objectives and performance outcomes
__ course outline that includes suggestions for multilevel classes
__ results from student needs assessment
__ record of emerging objectives from previous instruction
__ other:________________________

Comments

Action Plan/Next Steps

Score

0 1 2 3 NA

Priority

High Low

2. Curriculum and Instructional Materials

E. Curriculum and instructional materials are easily accessible, up to date, appropriate for adult learners, culturally sensitive, oriented to the language and literacy needs of the learners, and suitable for a variety of learning styles.

Measures

To score a 2 or 3, all the * measures should be in place.

Review of curriculum and instructional materials indicates that

*__1 They are up to date (e.g. published within the past 10 years).

*__2 They contain relevant content.

*__3 They take into account the linguistic and cultural diversity of the student population.

*__4 The layout and formatting (including size of font) is appropriate for the student population.

*__5 Visuals and graphics are clear, appropriate for adult learners, and culturally sensitive.

*__6 Voice and sound in audiovisual materials are clear and appropriate for adult learners.

*__7 The materials address a variety of learning styles by including the following exercises:

__ visual
__ aural
__ oral
__ manipulative, including drawing
__ kinesthetic

*__8 The materials are conducive to being used with a variety of grouping strategies.

__9 The materials contain exercises in which learners share previous experience with and prior knowledge of the content.

____ Other: ____________________

Action Plan/Next Steps

Sample Evidence

__ books
__ software
__ handouts
__ manipulatives
__ realia
__ audiovisual materials
__ other curriculum materials: _________
__ other:________________________

Comments

Score

0 1 2 3 NA

Priority

High Low

2. Curriculum and Instructional Materials

F. The program has an ongoing process for curriculum revision in response to the changing needs of the learners, community, and policies.

Measures

To score a 2 or 3, all the * measures should be in place.

*__1 Curriculum is reviewed or revised in one or more of the following ways:

- __ Curriculum is reviewed as part of a formal program review process that is regularly scheduled.
- __ Curriculum emerges from participatory activities between learners and the instructor.
- __ Program funds or seeks funding for curriculum projects targeted to specific or changing needs (e.g., integration of technology competencies into course outlines, development of curriculum for new semiliterate population, development of curriculum to meet the requirements of legislation in order to acquire government funding).

*__2 As part of the review process, the program seeks input from internal and external stakeholders, as appropriate.

__3 Faculty and staff contribute new curriculum materials to central resource area accessible to other instructors.

__4 Textbook committee meets regularly to select and approve new materials.

*__5 The curriculum review process includes steps to disseminate the materials throughout the program.

Action Plan/Next Steps

Sample Evidence

__ needs assessments
__ guidelines for curriculum review
__ minutes of curriculum meetings (date of last review meeting: ___________)
__ questionnaires or surveys
__ telephone notes
__ lists of participants and contributors in curriculum review process
__ memos
__ meeting agendas
__ schedule for textbook committee meetings (date of most recent meeting: _________)
__ other:_______________________

Comments

Score

0 1 2 3 NA

Priority

High Low

3. Instruction

A. Instructional activities adhere to principles of adult learning and language acquisition. These principles include the following:

- **Adult learners bring a variety of experiences, skills, and knowledge to the classroom that need to be acknowledged and included in lessons.**
- **Language acquisition is facilitated through providing a nonthreatening environment in which learners feel comfortable and self-confident and are encouraged to take risks to use the target language.**
- **Adult learners progress more rapidly when the content is relevant to their lives.**
- **Language learning is cyclical, not linear, so learning objectives need to be recycled in a variety of contexts.**

Measures

To score a 2 or 3, all the * measures should be in place.

*__1 Lesson plan formats and classroom activities offer learners an opportunity to share their prior knowledge of the language or content to be studied and practiced.

*__2 Instructional activities resemble activities in the learners' lives or prepare learners for relevant use of the language (e.g., the alphabet is taught in the context of spelling one's name over the telephone, not through memorization of isolated letters).

*__3 Instructional activities include methods, such as the language experience approach, which use the learners' lives as content and provide a context for the integration of listening, speaking, reading, and writing skill development.

*__4 Instructional activities make learners feel relaxed and comfortable and not afraid to use the language. Strategies that facilitate this include any of the following:

- __ friendly demeanor on behalf of the instructor
- __ use of humor in the classroom
- __ positive feedback to learners
- __ appropriate sequencing of instructional activities, such as comprehension activities before production

*__5 Instructional activities provide opportunities for learners to practice previously learned language patterns in different contexts in order to support the cyclical nature of language learning.

__6 Learners are encouraged to take risks through real communication activities. The instructor intervenes only to facilitate communication.

___ Other: ______________________

Action Plan/Next Steps

Sample Evidence

__ classroom observations
__ lesson plans
__ interviews with instructors
__ interviews with learners
__ teacher training materials
__ evaluations of instructors, including evaluations from students
__ other: ______________________

Comments

Score

0 1 2 3 NA

Priority

High Low

3. Instruction

B. Instructional approaches are varied to meet the needs of adult learners with diverse educational and cultural backgrounds. Examples of these approaches include, but are not limited to, the following:

___ grammar based
___ competency based or functional context
___ whole language
___ participatory
___ content based
___ project based

Measures

To score a 2 or 3, all the measures should be in place.

___1 Instructional approaches are selected according to learner goals or learner profiles (e.g., a grammar-based approach may be used to help a group of learners preparing for the TOEFL. A participatory approach may be used when learners bring a special language need to the classroom from a situation in the community).

___2 Different approaches are used at different times during a lesson to accommodate learner needs.

___3 Instructors can identify the instructional approaches they use and the rationale according to the needs of their learners.

____ Other: ____________________

Action Plan/Next Steps

Sample Evidence

__ description of the ESL program
__ classroom observations
__ lesson plans
__ lesson syllabi
__ interviews with instructors
__ interviews with learners
__ methodology training materials for faculty
__ other: ____________________

Comments

Score

0 1 2 3 NA

Priority

High Low

3. Instruction

C. Instructional activities engage the learners in taking an active role in the learning process.

Measures

To score a 2 or 3, the following measure should be in place.

___1 Learners take an active role in the learning process by doing one or more of the following:

- __ Learners complete exercises requiring active listening skills.
- __ Learners communicate with each other or the instructor on a regular basis in the classroom.
- __ Learners ask questions or request clarification in discussions or presentations.
- __ Learners revise and edit written assignments as part of the writing process.
- __ Learners engage in tasks in which they research information and then share it with others.
- __ Learners participate in the process of identifying course objectives.
- __ Learners have roles in class management tasks (e.g., helping new students).
- __ Learners document their own progress in meeting those objectives.

___ Other: ______________________

Sample Evidence

- __ classroom observations
- __ lesson plans
- __ interviews with Instructors
- __ interviews with learners
- __ learner role assignments listed on charts
- __ learner self-evaluations or portfolios
- __ other: ______________________

Comments

Action Plan/Next Steps

Score

0 1 2 3 NA

Priority

High Low

3. Instruction

D. Instructional activities focus on the acquisition of communication skills necessary for learners to function within the classroom, outside the classroom, or in other educational programs.

Measures

To score a 2 or 3, all the measures should be in place.

___1 The objectives for the lesson are transferable to real-life situations; instructional activities include practice and application of lessons to genuine real-life needs. Sample activities that demonstrate this include any of the following:

- __ role play
- __ pair practice
- __ classroom simulations
- __ small-group demonstrations
- __ contact assignments
- __ problem solving or problem posing

___2 In instructional activities, learners develop the functional language, content, and vocabulary necessary to communicate information in situations relevant to their goals (e.g., to pass the citizenship test, to get a job, to apply to college).

___ Other: ____________________

Action Plan/Next Steps

Sample Evidence

- __ classroom observation
- __ lesson plans
- __ interviews with instructors
- __ interviews with learners
- __ instructional materials
- __ learner portfolios
- __ log of classroom activities over several days
- __ other: __________________

Comments

Score

0 1 2 3 NA

Priority

High Low

3. Instruction

E. Instructional activities integrate the four language skills (listening, speaking, reading, and writing), focusing on receptive and productive skills appropriate to learners' needs.

Measures

To score a 2 or 3, all the measures should be in place.

___1 Instructional activities require or encourage the use of listening, speaking, reading, and writing skills.

___2 The listening, speaking, reading, and writing activities, where it is appropriate, are related to the same topic or content focus (e.g., if the focused outcome is telling a landlord about a housing problem, instructional activities focus on listening and speaking but can be extended to include writing skills with a note to the landlord).

___ Other: ____________________

Action Plan/Next Steps

Sample Evidence

__ classroom observation
__ lesson plans
__ interviews with instructors
__ interviews with learners
__ logs of classroom activities over several days
__ learner portfolios
__ instructional materials

Comments

Score

0 1 2 3 NA

Priority

High Low

3. Instruction

F. Instructional activities are varied to address the different learning styles (e.g., aural, oral, visual, kinesthetic) and special learning needs of the learners.

Measures

To score a 2 or 3, all the * measures should be in place.

*__1 A variety of learning modalities are addressed in a lesson:

__ visual
__ auditory/oral
__ kinesthetic

*__2 In presenting new information or language patterns to the learners, the instructor supports a verbal presentation with appropriate visuals or print materials and a physical demonstration.

*__3 Practice activities are varied and may include verbal interchanges among students, written exercises, hands-on manipulative tasks, simulations in which learners role play, or other activities addressing different learning modalities.

*__4 Assessment exercises to measure learner progress are also varied and may include verbal exercises, written exercises, manipulative tasks, or others.

__5 Learner styles may be identified using a simple, level-appropriate questionnaire or an oral interview.

___ Other:______________________

Sample Evidence

__ classroom observations
__ lesson plans
__ interviews with learners
__ classroom evaluations
__ interviews with instructors
__ logs of classroom activities over several days
__ instructional materials
__ learner portfolios
__ other: ________________

Comments

Action Plan/Next Steps

Score

0 1 2 3 NA

Priority

High Low

3. Instruction

G. Instructional activities incorporate grouping strategies and interactive tasks that facilitate the development of authentic communication skills. These include cooperative learning, information gap activities, role plays, simulations, problem solving, and problem posing.

Measures

To score a 2 or 3, the following measure should be in place.

___1 A classroom lesson includes grouping strategies or interactive tasks that facilitate authentic communication. The following are some examples of interactive tasks. One or more should be observed:

- __ In pair practice or information gap activities, learners practice the communication skills of asking questions, answering questions, and clarifying.
- __ In cooperative learning activities, learners work in pairs or small groups to complete tasks that require positive interdependence and cooperative skills, such as encouraging each other, agreeing and disagreeing, and reaching consensus.
- __ In problem solving activities, small groups practice communication skills, such as identifying the problem, discussing solutions, and analyzing consequences to the solutions.
- __ In a problem posing activity, learners interact to decide how to deal with a community problem or situation.
- __ In role play or simulation activities, learners interact with each other, choosing the correct language functions for their roles and situations.

____ Other:____________________

Action Plan/Next Steps

Sample Evidence

__ classroom observations
__ lesson plans
__ interviews with learners
__ interviews with teacher
__ logs of classroom activities over several days
__ reviews of instructional materials
__ other: ______________

Comments

Score

0 1 2 3 NA

Priority

High Low

3. Instruction

H. Instructional activities take into account the needs of multilevel groups of learners, particularly those with minimal literacy skills in their native language and English.

Measures

To score a 2 or 3, one or more of the following measures should be in place.

One or more of the following strategies is used to accommodate the needs of multilevel groups of learners:

___1 Within a class session, learners are grouped at different times to do different level-specific activities (e.g., one group practices naming letters of the alphabet or decoding consonant sounds while another group completes a written exercise).

___2 Within a class, learners use different materials according to their literacy levels (e.g., different levels of the same text or workbook series).

___3 Learners with special needs are given special worksheets prepared by the instructor.

___4 Learners of different ability levels work together so that higher level learners can assist lower level learners with a learning task.

___5 A volunteer or teacher's aide periodically works with individuals or small groups of learners with special literacy needs.

___6 Learners are pulled out of a class for special tutoring in literacy; when appropriate, native language instruction can bridge the development of literacy skills in English.

___ Other:______________________

Action Plan/Next Steps

Sample Evidence

__ classroom observations
__ interviews with instructors
__ interviews with learners
__ lesson plans
__ classroom schedule of activities with different groups of learners
__ other:______________________

Comments

Score

0 1 2 3 NA

Priority

High Low

3. Instruction

I. Instructional activities focus on the development of language and culturally appropriate behaviors needed for critical thinking, problem solving, team participation, and study skills.

Measures

To score a 2 or 3, all the measures should be in place.

Instructional activities are facilitated so that

___1 Learners acquire and practice the language patterns required to apply their critical thinking skills. Examples of critical thinking skills are the following:
- __ comparison and contrast
- __ generalization with examples
- __ use of the conditional to analyze
- __ summarization/making conclusions
- __ expression of feelings or judgments

___2 Learners use the appropriate language patterns and cultural behaviors to solve problems in the classroom or problems related to their daily lives. They follow the steps of identifying the problem, possible solutions, consequences to those solutions, and selecting the best solution according to the situation.

___3 Learners practice the language and behaviors needed to work effectively in teams. For example, they collaborate with shared resources, take on role assignments, negotiate with each other, encourage each other, and practice active listening skills.

___4 Learners participate in activities that strengthen their study skills. Examples of possible activities include the following:
- __ organizing their learning materials
- __ practicing note taking
- __ practicing outlining
- __ practicing test taking
- __ documenting their own progress
- __ completing homework assignments
- __ practicing English outside the classroom
- __ researching information through technology
- __ other: ___________

___ Other:_______________

Action Plan/Next Steps

Sample Evidence

- __ classroom observations
- __ interviews with Instructors
- __ interviews with learners
- __ lesson plans
- __ other: ____________________

Comments

Score

0 1 2 3 NA

Priority

High Low

3. Instruction

J. Instructional activities give learners opportunities to use authentic resources both inside and outside the classroom.

Measures

To score a 2 or 3, one or more of the following measures should be in place.

___1 Learners acquire language skills within the classroom by using resources from the real world. Examples include the following:
- __ phone books
- __ newspapers
- __ magazines
- __ school notices
- __ community bulletins or announcements
- __ video programs
- __ literature
- __ recorded audio messages
- __ recorded music
- __ television or radio
- __ employment handbooks or policy manuals
- __ other:_____________

___2 Learners have opportunities to communicate with people in the community or workplace in one or more of the following ways:
- __ guest speakers are invited
- __ students take field trips
- __ students complete contact assignments outside of class
- __ other: _________

___3 Learners have opportunities to acquire information from the Internet within the classroom or receive assignments to do so outside the classroom.

____ Other:________________

Action Plan/Next Steps

Sample Evidence

- __ classroom observations
- __ lesson plans
- __ interviews with instructors
- __ interviews with learners
- __ classroom materials
- __ log of classroom activities
- __ other: _____________________

Comments

Score

0 1 2 3 NA

Priority

High Low

3. Instruction

K. Instructional activities give learners opportunities to develop awareness of and competency in the use of appropriate technologies to meet lesson objectives.

Measures

To score a 2 or 3, all the measures should be in place.

___1 Learners have opportunities to fulfill lesson objectives through the use of technology, such as any of the following:

- __ telephone
- __ fax machine
- __ copy machine
- __ computer in classroom or lab
- __ audiotape recorder
- __ video equipment
- __ digital camera
- __ language master machine
- __ on-line distance education technology
- __ overhead projector
- __ other: ___________________

___2 In the process of using technology, learners are taught the language or terminology associated with it as appropriate to level in order to operate it, follow instructions, report problems, ask for assistance, or explain the use of the equipment to others.

___ Other:_______________________

Action Plan/Next Steps

Sample Evidence

- __ classroom observations
- __ lesson plans
- __ interviews with instructors
- __ interviews with learners
- __ student projects using technology
- __ classroom assignments using technology
- __ other: _____________________

Comments

Score

0 1 2 3 NA

Priority

High Low

3. Instruction

L. Instructional activities are culturally sensitive to the learners and integrate language and culture.

Measures

To score a 2 or 3, all the measures should be in place.

___1 Instructional activities teach about U.S. culture and its differences from other cultures.

___2 The instructor's teaching style and behaviors, including the use of gestures, is sensitive to the customs and cultural norms of the learners.

___3 Instructional activities encourage the learners to learn about and share each other's cultures (e.g., students may take turns giving presentations about their countries).

___4 Instructional activities do not require learners to do things that are forbidden by their cultures or religious preferences (e.g., members of the opposite sex making public physical contact or eating foods, such as pork).

___ Other:______________________

Action Plan/Next Steps

Sample Evidence

__ class observations
__ interviews with learners
__ lesson plans
__ interviews with instructors
__ written policies or guidelines on cultural considerations
__ other: ____________________

Comments

Score

0 1 2 3 NA

Priority

High Low

3. Instruction

M. Instructional activities prepare learners for formal and informal assessment situations, such as test taking, job interviews, and keeping personal learning records.

Measures

To score a 2 or 3, all the * measures should be in place.

*__1 In classroom activities or on weekly tests, learners complete exercises similar to those found on standardized or required tests (e.g., multiple-choice items, true-false items, essay questions). The instructor teaches learners how to complete a variety of test item types.

*__2 During testing situations, the teacher enforces typical testing requirements (e.g., no talking, no helping each other, keeping adequate distance between learners).

*__3 In role play activities or simulations, learners practice interview situations they will encounter outside the classroom (e.g., for jobs or citizenship interviews).

__4 When learners receive assessment results, the teacher guides them in recording the results on a chart or in a folder with which learners can periodically monitor their progress.

__5 Personal learning records of learners contain test scores or samples of learners' work that indicate monitoring of progress by the learners themselves.

__6 Instructors introduce or discuss purposes for standardized testing with learners using simple, level-appropriate language or visuals (e.g, instructor draws a mind map on "why test?" and includes answers elicited from learners, e.g., "for learners, teachers, funding").

___ Other: ______________________

Action Plan/Next Steps

Sample Evidence

__ class observations
__ interviews with learners
__ interviews with instructors
__ assessment materials and records
__ personal learning records
__ learner portfolios
__ learner self-evaluations
__ lesson plans
__ other: ______________________

Comments

Score

0 1 2 3 NA

Priority

High Low

4. Learner Recruitment, Intake, and Orientation

A. A quality ESL program has effective procedures for identifying and recruiting adult English learners. The procedures include strategies for collecting data on community demographics that identify the populations that need to be served, particularly those at the lowest level of literacy and knowledge of English.

Measures

To score a 2 or 3, one or more of the following measures should be in place.

The program identifies the learners that need to be served by doing one or more of the following:

___1 reviews census data to identify the learner population

___2 reviews results of national literacy surveys to identify levels of literacy within the local area and the numbers to be served (see NALS, 1993)

___3 reviews community demographic reports (e.g., newspaper articles describing population trends)

___4 compares enrollment and attendance patterns from year to year to identify new trends in enrollment

___5 meets and communicates with local refugee resettlement agencies

___6 networks with K–12 schools in the local area to compare population statistics (e.g., number of adults, parents, children)

___7 maintains communication with immigration agency or reads immigration updates to keep abreast of new legislation that may affect student enrollment

___8 networks with local ethnic and religious organizations

___ Other:_______________

Action Plan/Next Steps

Sample Evidence

__ analysis of census reports
__ community demographic reports
__ NALS report, 1993
__ minutes from meetings
__ program summary reports
__ accreditation reports
__ newspaper articles on community demographics
__ e-mail messages
__ publicity flyers and outreach materials
__ data on results of recruitment
__ other: _______________

Comments

Score

0 1 2 3 NA

Priority

High Low

4. Learner Recruitment, Intake, and Orientation

B. The program uses a variety of recruitment strategies.

Measures

To score a 2 or 3, two or more of the following strategies should be in place.

Program recruitment strategies effectively reach local communities through two or more of the following ways:

___1 Recruitment is done directly by the program through
  __ fliers
  __ spots on TV or radio
  __ signs or banners
  __ newspapers
  __ mailer inserts
  __ other:______________

___2 Information about the program is made available through a referral network (e.g., employment offices, human services, refugee resettlement agencies, ethnic and religious organizations).

___3 Recruitment drives are held at public events.

___4 Announcements of classes (in native languages or English) are sent home with children in K–12 schools.

___5 Ads and information are placed in community and organizational news bulletins and fliers.

___6 Student-to-new-student recruitment efforts are organized (e.g., bring a friend to school campaigns).

___ Other: ________________

Action Plan/Next Steps

Sample Evidence

__ recruiting and outreach materials
__ publicity for recruitment
__ schedule of recruitment activities

List recruitment methods used:

____

____

Comments

Score

0 1 2 3 NA

Priority

High Low

4. Learner Recruitment, Intake, and Orientation

C. The program takes steps to ensure that culturally and linguistically appropriate recruitment and program information materials and activities reach the appropriate populations in multiple languages as needed.

Measures

To score a 2 or 3, all measures should be in place.

___1 Recruitment materials and strategies are in native languages of the predominant student populations.

___2 Recruitment materials and strategies are suitable for persons with special needs (e.g., include large print, audiotapes).

___3 Recruitment materials and strategies are reviewed by members of the target population for the following:

__ accuracy
__ culturally appropriate content and methods
__ clarity
__ appropriateness for individuals with special needs

Action Plan/Next Steps

Sample Evidence

__ list of recruitment activities
__ recruitment materials translated into different languages
__ program information material
__ notes or records of reviews of materials
__ other: ____________________

Comments

Score

0 1 2 3 NA

Priority

High Low

4. Learner Recruitment, Intake, and Orientation

D. The program evaluates the effectiveness of its recruitment efforts and makes changes as needed.

Measures

To score a 2 or 3, all the measures should be in place.

___1 The program keeps track of success rates of recruitment strategies by doing any of the following:

- __ documents which events draw new learners
- __ documents which communities/ populations are missing, based on demographic analysis
- __ surveys enrolled learners about how they found out about the program and tallies the results
- __ enlists learner expertise or participation in designing recruitment strategies

___2 The program conducts periodic reviews/ evaluations of recruitment strategies and makes appropriate adjustments.

Sample Evidence

__ recruitment evaluation report
__ minutes from meetings
__ learner surveys
__ records of results of recruitment efforts
__ other: ______________________

Comments

Action Plan/Next Steps

Score

0 1 2 3 NA

Priority

High Low

4. Learner Recruitment, Intake, and Orientation

E. The program has an intake process that provides appropriate assessment of learners' needs, goals, and language proficiency levels; an orientation process that provides learners with information about the program; and, if needed, a procedure for referring learners to support services within the program or through other agencies and for accommodating learners waiting to enter the program.

Measures

To score a 2 or 3, all * measures should be in place.

*__1 During the intake process, the program collects the following:
- __ demographic information, such as learner
- __ country of origin
- __ age
- __ language background
- __ prior educational background, including literacy in native language
- __ current or prior work experience
- __ needs and goals of learner
- __ English language proficiency levels in
  - __listening
  - __speaking
  - __reading
  - __writing
- __ need for support services
- __ other:____________

*__2 This information is collected prior to enrollment or in class as part of the registration procedures through one or more of the following ways (in English or the native language):
- __ one-to-one interview with student
- __ registration form
- __ needs assessment form
- __ student profile form
- __ other: ______________

__3 Procedures for assessing English language proficiency levels may include one or more of the following:
- __ oral interviews
- __ writing sample
- __ program-developed placement test
- __ standardized proficiency test
- __ other: ______________

Continued on p. 99

4. Learner Recruitment, Intake, and Orientation

E. *Continued*

Measures *(continued)*

*__4 As part of the intake process, learners are oriented to the program through one or more of the following procedures:
- __ Learners receive written information about the program in their native language.
- __ Learners view a short videotape in their native language or English.
- __ Learners attend a short orientation session.
- __ Learners receive information about the program from their teacher during class time.
- __ Other: ________________

*__5 If classes are filled, the program uses a procedure to accommodate learners waiting to enter; this may include one or more of the following:
- __ provides simple written instructions to a learners as to when they can enroll
- __ calls learners on the waiting list when openings occur
- __ enrolls the learner in a temporary orientation class until an opening in the regular program occurs
- __ refers the learners to a distance learning class
- __ refers the learners to a learning lab for individualized study until an opening occurs in a regular classroom
- __ refers to other programs

____ Other:______________________

Action Plan/Next Steps

Sample Evidence

- __ written procedures for intake
- __ forms used for intake, such as student profile forms, tests
- __ needs assessment forms
- __ support services referral form
- __ interviews with instructors and support staff
- __ orientation materials
- __ agenda of orientation activities
- __ interviews with learners
- __ waiting list
- __ referral policies
- __ list of agencies to which referrals can be made
- __ language level assessment materials
- __ other: ________________

Comments

Score

0 1 2 3 NA

Priority

High Low

5. Learner Retention and Transition

A. The program supports retention through enrollment and attendance procedures that reflect program goals, requirements of program funders, and demands on the adult learner.

Measures

To score a 2 or 3, all * measures should be in place.

__1 Program coordinators analyze enrollment and attendance patterns of each class in order to evaluate factors that improve or limit retention.

*__2 The program supports learner retention by one or more of the following strategies:

__ Instruction is offered at different times of the day to accommodate learners' schedules.

__ Classes of different lengths or intensity are offered.

__ Short-term and long-term classes are offered (e.g., 6-week classes, 12-week classes, 18-week classes)

*__3 The initial enrollment/registration process is user friendly and efficient.

*__4 The program maintains class sizes that support learner retention.

___ Other:____________________

Action Plan/Next Steps

Sample Evidence

__ class schedule
__ written attendance policies
__ enrollment procedures and forms
__ interviews with learners
__ class size records
__ interviews with program coordinators or administrators
__ other:______________________

Comments

Score

0 1 2 3 NA

Priority

High Low

5. Learner Retention and Transition

B. The program encourages learners to participate consistently and long enough to reach their identified goals. This may be accomplished by adjusting the scheduling and location of classes and by providing appropriate support services.

Measures

To score a 2 or 3, all * measures should be in place.

*__1 The program provides each learner with an orientation to the school or class.

*__2 The program facilitates activities for learners to set goals and monitor their progress toward meeting those goals.

__3 The program provides support services such as the following:

- __ childcare or access to childcare
- __ transportation to and from class
- __ counseling to guide learners through the program
- __ tutoring or aide assistance in classes as needed (e.g., to help learners with lower literacy levels)

__4 The program provides distance learning courses for learners unable to attend regular classes.

__5 The program provides on-line courses.

Action Plan/Next Steps

Sample Evidence

- __ class schedule
- __ learner orientation plan and schedule
- __ list of support services provided and contact information (if not on site)
- __ list of on-line courses and distance learning classes available
- __ interviews with learners
- __ other: ______________________

Comments

Score

0 1 2 3 NA

Priority

High Low

5. Learner Retention and Transition

C. The program accommodates the special needs of learners as fully as possible.

Measures

To score a 2 or 3, the following measure should be in place.

____ The program accommodates the special needs of learners in one or more of the following ways:

- __ case management
- __ counseling
- __ native language support
- __ providing learning accommodations (e.g., magnifiers for learners with visual impairment, interpreters for learners with hearing impairment)

Action Plan/Next Steps

Sample Evidence

- __ interviews with learners
- __ program audit documenting accommodation of special needs
- __ other: ________________

Comments

Score

0 1 2 3 NA

Priority

High Low

5. Learner Retention and Transition

D. The program contacts learners with irregular attendance patterns and acknowledges learners who attend regularly.

Measures

To score a 2 or 3, all * measures should be in place.

*__1 The program contacts learners with irregular attendance patterns to encourage re-entry.

__2 The program rewards learners for excellent attendance, making progress, completing courses, and fulfilling their goals within the program through the awarding of certificates or special ceremonies.

___ Other: ____________________

Action Plan/Next Steps

Sample Evidence

__ phone logs
__ sample letters
__ interviews with learners
__ recognition certificates
__ other: ____________________

Comments

Score

0 1 2 3 NA

Priority

High Low

5. Learner Retention and Transition

E. The program provides learners with appropriate support for transition to other programs.

Measures

To score a 2 or 3, all measures should be in place.

___1 The program facilitates the efficient transfer of learners to other classes or programs in order to meet learner needs.

___2 The program supports transition through one or more of the following:

- __ provides information about other programs
- __ provides counseling
- __ provides documentation of learner outcomes that is recognized by other programs
- __ refers learners to other programs
- __ provides guest speakers to talk about other programs
- __ facilitates field trips to other programs
- __ other:________________

Action Plan/Next Steps

Sample Evidence

- __ exit interviews
- __ interviews with counselors
- __ record of transfers within program
- __ schedule of speakers, field trips
- __ minutes of meetings
- __ description of other educational options
- __ other: ____________________

Comments

Score

0 1 2 3 NA

Priority

High Low

6. Assessment and Learner Gains

Assessment Policy

A. The program has a comprehensive assessment policy.

Measures

To score a 2 or 3, all the measures should be in place.

The policy has the following attributes:

___1 reflects the mission and goals of the program

___2 accommodates legal requirements

___3 reflects the needs of the learners and other stakeholders

___4 is linked to instructional objectives and activities

___5 is developed with input from internal and external stakeholders

___6 is based on principles of adult learning, second language acquisition, language learning pedagogy, literacy development for adults, and sound language testing principles and procedures

___ Other: ______________________

Action Plan/Next Steps

Sample Evidence

__ program guidelines
__ course outlines
__ grant guidelines
__ state funding guidelines or policies
__ teacher training materials
__ interviews with program staff
__ accreditation self-study
__ program audit reports
__ other: ______________________

Comments

Score

0 1 2 3 NA

Priority

High Low

6. Assessment and Learner Gains

Assessment Policy

B. The program has a process for assessing learners' skills and goals for placement into the program, documentation of progress within the program, and exit from the program. This includes appropriate assessment of learners with special learning needs.

Measures

To score a 2 or 3, all the * measures should be in place.

The program has a process for the following:

*__1 assessing learners' needs and goals for placement into the program

*__2 documenting progress within the program

*__3 documenting criteria for exit from the program

___4 assessing learners with special needs

Sample Evidence

__ guidelines for testing
__ sample assessments or tests
__ interviews with staff
__ assessment reports
__ other: ______________________

Comments

Action Plan/Next Steps

Score

0 1 2 3 NA

Priority

High Low

6. Assessment and Learner Gains

Assessment Policy

C. Assessment activities are ongoing and appropriately scheduled.

Measures

To score a 2 or 3, all the measures should be in place.

___1 Multiple opportunities for assessment occur during the course of instruction.

___2 Assessment activities are scheduled at suitable times to meet learner and program needs.

Sample Evidence

__ schedules for assessment

Comments

Action Plan/Next Steps

Score

0 1 2 3 NA

Priority

High Low

6. Assessment and Learner Gains

Assessment Policy

D. The program has procedures for collecting and reporting data on educational gains and outcomes.

Measures

To score a 2 or 3, all the measures should be in place.

The program has and follows procedures for:

___1 collecting and reporting data on educational gains and outcomes

___2 reporting data without violating standards of confidentiality

___3 reporting data in clear and precise language to all stakeholders

Sample Evidence

__ assessment reports
__ written record-keeping policies and procedures
__ data collection instruments or software

Comments

Action Plan/Next Steps

Score

0 1 2 3 NA

Priority

High Low

6. Assessment and Learner Gains

Assessment Policy

E. The program provides appropriate facilities, equipment, supplies, and personnel for assessment activities.

Measures

To score a 2 or 3, all the measures should be in place.

___1 Facilities for assessment have all the following characteristics:

- __ spacious (e.g., there is sufficient distance between learners during assessment)
- __ well lighted
- __ sufficiently quiet
- __ appropriately ventilated
- __ accessible to disabled learners
- __ equipped with appropriate tables and chairs for testing purposes
- __ equipped with a board or place to post general directions and time limits for assessment activities
- __ other:_________________

___2 Testers in assessment situations are

- __ trained to ensure that learners understand all testing procedures
- __ informed about the purpose of the test
- __ trained to administer the tests according to manual or assessment guidelines
- __ available to monitor the testing environment for test security and integrity

Sample Evidence

- __ observation of assessment facilities
- __ accreditation reports
- __ equipment used for assessment
- __ observation of assessment activities
- __ interviews with students
- __ interviews with teachers
- __ interview with testing staff
- __ other: ___________________

- __ observation of training
- __ training materials
- __ training evaluations

Continued on p. 110

6. Assessment and Learner Gains

Assessment Policy

E. *Continued*

Measures *(continued)*

___3 Testing materials are not damaged or marked.

___4 Testing materials are kept in a secure location.

___5 Audiovisual, computer, or other technology equipment required for testing works well.

Sample Evidence *(continued)*

__ materials used for testing

__ observation of equipment used for testing

Comments

Action Plan/Next Steps

Score

0 1 2 3 NA

Priority

High Low

6. Assessment and Learner Gains

Types of Assessment

F. The program identifies learners' needs and goals as individuals, family members, community participants, workers, and lifelong learners.

Measures

To score a 2 or 3, all the measures should be in place.

___1 Individual student learning records list learner goals and interests.

___2 Learner needs assessments are conducted initially and on an ongoing basis.

___3 School assessment reports tally learners' needs and goals to identify program needs.

___ Other: ____________________

Sample Evidence

__ learner needs assessment forms
__ school assessment reports
__ interviews with learners
__ learner portfolios
__ individual student learning records
__ other: ______________________

Comments

Action Plan/Next Steps

Score

0 1 2 3 NA

Priority

High Low

6. Assessment and Learner Gains

Types of Assessment

G. The program assesses the language proficiency levels of learners in the areas of listening, speaking, reading, and writing. The assessments may also identify learners' literacy skills in their primary language and any learning disabilities.

Measures

To score a 2 or 3, both of the measures below should be in place.

___1 Individual student learning records list proficiency levels through formal or informal assessment in at least two of the following:

___listening:

___informal ___formal

Name of instrument: ________________

___speaking:

___informal ___formal

Name of instrument: ________________

___reading:

___informal ___formal

Name of instrument: ________________

___writing:

___informal ___formal

Name of instrument: ________________

___Primary language literacy

___informal ___formal

Name of instrument: ________________

___2 As appropriate, special needs are indicated in learner records (e.g., dyslexia, short-term memory problem)

Action Plan/Next Steps

Sample Evidence

__ learner portfolios or learning records
__ sample assessment materials
__ assessment procedures and guidelines
__ assessment tools
__ assessment reports
__ other: ________________

Comments

Score

0 1 2 3 NA

Priority

High Low

6. Assessment and Learner Gains

Types of Assessment

H. The program uses a variety of appropriate assessments, including authentic, performance-based assessments; standardized tests; learner self-assessment; and assessment of nonlinguistic outcomes (e.g., perceived improvement in self-esteem, participation in teamwork activities). Standardized assessment instruments are valid and reliable, based on studies with the targeted adult-level population.

Measures

To score a 2 or 3, all the measures should be in place.

___1 Individual learner records include the following information on students (* = highly recommended):

*__ placement
*__ progress
__ diagnosis of skills
*__ achievement
__ nonlinguistic outcomes
*__ program or level exit

___2 Individual records indicate a variety of assessments are used, such as two or more of the following:

__ writing samples
__ a portfolio of student work
__ textbook progress/completion tests
__ weekly unit test from a text or teacher developed
__ teacher-made, criterion-referenced progress and exit tests
__ self-appraised progress on pre- and post-surveys
__ program-developed pre- and postassessments based on curriculum
__ performance-based tests
__ checklist of documented outcomes
__ checklist of completed competencies correlated to learner needs
__ learner's log or journal
__ oral interview with learner
__ teacher observation checklist
__ standardized tests
__ other:________________

Continued on p. 114

6. Assessment and Learner Gains

Types of Assessment

H. ***Continued***

Measures *(continued)*

___3 If standardized assessment instruments are used, both of the following are in place:

- __ The assessment instrument has accompanying information on reliability and validity studies that have been done with the test.
- __ Accompanying documentation indicates that the studies were conducted with the targeted adult-level population of nonnative speakers of English.

Sample Evidence

- __ student learning records
- __ student portfolios
- __ sample assessment instruments
- __ assessment data reports
- __ interviews with staff

Comments

Action Plan/Next Steps

Score

0 1 2 3 NA

Priority

High Low

6. Assessment and Learner Gains

Uses of Assessment

I. The information obtained through needs assessment is used to aid administrators, teachers, and tutors in developing curricula, materials, skills assessments, and teaching approaches that are relevant to learners' lives.

Measures

To score a 2 or 3, all the measures should be in place.

Results from the needs assessment process are

___1 considered in the selection of materials and teaching approaches

___2 used in the development or revision of curriculum

___3 used to identify learners' special interests and needs

___4 used to set instructional priorities in the program (e.g, offer more VESL courses to accommodate learners waiting to get jobs)

___5 used to develop new courses or types of ESL classes (e.g., pronunciation, writing)

___ Other:__________________

Sample Evidence

__ needs assessment forms
__ interviews with teachers
__ teaching manual or guidelines
__ interview with administrator
__ assessment forms
__ minutes from planning meetings, trainings, or curriculum meetings

Comments

Action Plan/Next Steps

Score

0 1 2 3 NA

Priority

High Low

6. Assessment and Learner Gains

Uses of Assessment

J. Assessment results are clearly explained and shared with learners, to the extent permitted by assessment guidelines, in order to help learners progress.

Measures

To score a 2 or 3, all the * measures should be in place.

*__1 The results of all assessments are

- __ explained to the learners
- __ used to counsel learners
- __ posted or recorded on permanent records so that they can be accessed by learners at a later date
- __ other:___________________

*__2 The rules of confidentiality are respected in the sharing of results.

__3 Assessment results are linked to special recognition, such as certificates of progress or completion.

Action Plan/Next Steps

Sample Evidence

- __ interviews with learners
- __ student learning records
- __ assessment reports
- __ charts illustrating assessment results correlated with levels
- __ keys explaining assessment results
- __ certificates documenting learner assessment results
- __ written confidentiality and reporting policies
- __ other: ________________________

Comments

Score

0 1 2 3 NA

Priority

High Low

6. Assessment and Learner Gains

Uses of Assessment

K. Assessment activities document learners' progress within the ESL program toward advancement to other training programs, employment, postsecondary education, and attainment of other educational goals.

Measures

To score a 2 or 3, all the measures should be in place.

___1 Learners are informed of the assessment requirements for entrance into other programs (e.g., job training, postsecondary education).

___2 Learners are continually informed as to how their progress on assessments relates to advancement within the ESL program and to other programs.

___3 Results from assessment activities are used to place learners in

- __ technical or vocational programs
- __ higher levels of ESL instruction
- __ other education programs
- __ employment
- __ other:__________________

___4 The program documents and reports the number of learners who achieve significant learning gains or advance to other programs on a regular basis.

Sample Evidence

- __ assessment reports
- __ assessment requirements of other programs
- __ students' learning records
- __ surveys of learners
- __ transcripts
- __ records of transfers and advancement within program
- __ exit interviews
- __ documentation of the following:
  - ___% achieved significant learning gains
  - ___% promoted to higher levels
  - ___% got jobs or better jobs
  - ___% entered vocational programs
  - ___% entered postsecondary programs
  - ___% __________________
  - __ other:__________________

Comments

Action Plan/Next Steps

Score

0 1 2 3 NA

Priority

High Low

6. Assessment and Learner Gains

Uses of Assessment

L. Results of assessment provide information about educational gains and learner outcomes and provide the basis for recommendations for further assessment (e.g., special needs, literacy considerations).

Measures

To score a 2 or 3, one or more of the following measures should be in place:

___1 Learner assessment results are reviewed by instructional staff, and, if appropriate, learners are referred to other segments of the program or referred for further assessment.

___2 Program staff tally learner assessment results to document learner gains and outcomes and review these statistics regularly.

___3 Assessment results recorded in individual learner portfolios document educational gains or achievement of learner outcomes.

___ Other:________________________

Action Plan/Next Steps

Sample Evidence

__ learner assessment records
__ assessment reports
__ interviews with instructors
__ referral forms to special services
__ other:________________________

Comments

Score

0 1 2 3 NA

Priority

High Low

6. Assessment and Learner Gains

Learner Gains

M. The program has a process by which learners identify and demonstrate progress toward or attainment of their short- and long-term goals.

Measures

To score a 2 or 3, all the measures should be in place.

___1 Learner goals are recorded in one or more of the following ways:
- __ Learners record their short- and long-term goals during the placement process on student profile forms.
- __ Learners identify their goals during classroom exercises facilitated by the instructor.
- __ Learners record their goals in individual portfolios used for assessment.
- __ Learners record their goals on testing forms.
- __ Learners record their goals in journals
- __ Other:________________

___2 Learners' progress toward attainment of goals is recorded in one or more of the following ways:
- __ on learner profile forms used for placement
- __ in individual portfolios used in the classroom
- __ on testing forms
- __ on exercise papers used during instruction
- __ in learners' journals
- __ other: ________________

___3 The program has a system to document and report the short- and long-term goals of its learners.

___4 The attainment of learner goals is tallied on cumulative school reports and reported to interested stakeholders.

Action Plan/Next Steps

Sample Evidence

- __ learner needs assessment forms
- __ learner profile or placement forms
- __ school assessment reports
- __ learner portfolios or learning records
- __ interviews with learners
- __ class observations
- __ testing forms
- __ learners' journals
- __ other: ________________

Comments

Score

0 1 2 3 NA

Priority

High Low

6. Assessment and Learner Gains

Learner Gains

N. The program has a process by which learners demonstrate skill-level improvements in listening (L), speaking (S), reading (R), and writing (W) through a variety of assessments.

Measures

To score a 2 or 3, the following measure should be in place.

___1 Review of learner records indicates improvement demonstrated using more than one of the following measures:

- __ standardized pre-/posttest score gains
  ___L ___S ___R ___W
- __ learner portfolio with verification of completed tasks or skills
  ___L ___S ___R ___W
- __ performance assessment results with criteria that define successful skill attainment or completion of outcomes
  ___L ___S ___R ___W
- __ pre-/postwriting samples with assessment criteria and results attached
- __ weekly tests (from textbooks or teacher developed)
  ___L ___S ___R ___W
- __ learner self-appraised progress on pre-/postsurveys
  ___L ___S ___R ___W
- __ criterion-referenced progress or level exit tests
  ___L ___S ___R ___W

___ Other: ____________________

Action Plan/Next Steps

Sample Evidence

- __ learning records
- __ cumulative test score reports
- __ pre-/postsurveys
- __ writing samples
- __ samples of assessment materials
- __ learner portfolios
- __ assessment reports
- __ learner self-evaluations
- __ observations
- __ other: ____________________

Comments

Score

0 1 2 3 NA

Priority

High Low

6. Assessment and Learner Gains

Learner Gains

O. The program has a process by which learners demonstrate progress in nonlinguistic areas identified as important toward meeting their goals.

Measures

To score a 2 or 3, all the measures should be in place.

___1 Progress in nonlinguistic outcomes is indicated through one or more of the following:

__ learner journal
__ learner self-assessment pre-/postquestionnaire
__ teacher observation checklist
__ learner interviews
__ other: ________________

___2 Nonlinguistic outcomes that are documented include any of the following:

__ increased confidence
__ increased participation in class
__ increased use of resources
__ improved study habits
__ increased participation in community or other activities outside of class
__ other:________________

Action Plan/Next Steps

Sample Evidence

__ learner journals
__ learner self-assessment questionnaires
__ classroom observation checklists
__ interviews with learners
__ anecdotes from students
__ other: ________________

Comments

Score

0 1 2 3 NA

Priority

High Low

7. Employment Conditions and Staffing

Employment Conditions

A. The program supports compensation and benefits commensurate with those of instructional and other professional staff with comparable positions and qualifications within similar institutions.

Measures

To score a 2 or 3, all the measures should be in place.

___1 Within funding or institutional guidelines, the program works toward providing full-time employment to its instructional staff.

% instructors with full-time employment: ___
% instructors with part-time employment: ___

___2 Within funding or institutional guidelines, the program works toward providing benefits for all staff, including any of the following:

__ health insurance
__ vision insurance
__ dental insurance
__ life insurance
__ paid professional leave
__ paid holidays
__ vacation leave
__ bereavement leave
__ personnel business leave (e.g., for cultural holidays)
__ sabbatical leave
__ maternity/paternity leave
__ workers' compensation
__ disability leave
__ retirement package
__ other: ________________

___3 The program supports compensation for noninstructional activities such as any of the following:
__ student conferences
__ special projects
__ preparation for instruction
__ attendance at staff development functions
__ faculty meetings
__ other: ________________

Sample Evidence

__ employee contracts
__ salary schedules
__ personnel records
__ assigned faculty teaching hours or human resource data
__ union agreements
__ interviews with faculty and staff
__ program budget
__ reports and memos documenting work toward improved compensation and benefits
__ documentation of the following statistics:
  __ % instructional staff with full time employment
  __ % instructional staff with part time employment

Continued on p. 123

7. Employment Conditions and Staffing

Employment Conditions

A. *Continued*

Measures *(continued)*

___4 The program provides a salary scale and promotional ladder.

___5 Full-time and part-time faculty have the same opportunity for promotion as other academic faculty or professional staff with comparable degrees and experience.

___ Other: ____________________

Sample Evidence *(continued)*

__ list of benefits provided for instructional and professional staff (check benefit; then check whether it applies to part-time or full-time employees or both):

Benefit		
__ health insurance	__p/t	__f/t
__ vision insurance	__p/t	__f/t
__ dental insurance	__p/t	__f/t
__ life insurance	__p/t	__f/t
__ paid professional leave	__p/t	__f/t
__ paid holidays	__p/t	__f/t
__ vacation leave	__p/t	__f/t
__ bereavement leave	__p/t	__f/t
__ personnel business leave (e.g., for cultural holidays)	__p/t	__f/t
__ sabbatical leave	__p/t	__f/t
__ maternity/ paternity leave	__p/t	__f/t
__ workers' compensation	__p/t	__f/t
__ disability/family medical leave	__p/t	__f/t
__ retirement package	__p/t	__f/t
__ other: ______________		

Comments

Action Plan/Next Steps

Score

0 1 2 3 NA

Priority

High Low

7. Employment Conditions and Staffing

Employment Conditions

B. The program has in place policies and procedures that ensure professional treatment of staff.

Measures

To score a 2 or 3, all the measures should be in place.

___1 The program supports negotiation with the faculty and staff to improve working conditions.

___2 All full-time and part-time staff receive timely appointment letters or contracts.

___3 All faculty are fully informed in writing of their employment prospects for the following term.

___4 Written policies are available to all staff.

___5 All faculty and staff have access to a grievance procedure.

___6 The program supports and complies with nondiscrimination and affirmative action guidelines.

___7 Faculty and staff receive sufficient advance notice for a change in work assignments.

___8 Reasonable notice is provided for class closures due to insufficient enrollment.

___9 The program provides all paid and volunteer instructional staff with written job descriptions.

__10 Full-time and part-time faculty are eligible for the same types of professional development support, including travel, release time, right to pursue grants, and right to participate in professional development events as received by other academic faculty or professional staff.

__11 The program provides clear criteria for dismissal.

__12 Seniority is one consideration in practices for continued employment or promotion.

____ Other: ______________________

Action Plan/Next Steps

Sample Evidence

__ union agreements
__ employment contracts
__ program rules and procedures
__ grievance forms and guidelines
__ sample form letters
__ interviews with staff
__ other: ________________

Comments

Score

0 1 2 3 NA

Priority

High Low

7. Employment Conditions and Staffing

Employment Conditions

C. The program supports a safe and clean working environment.

Measures

To score a 2 or 3, all the measures should be in place.

The program provides a safe and clean working environment by providing:

___1 adequate phone communication between learners, faculty and the institution's personnel

___2 adequate ventilation

___3 appropriate lighting

___4 regular custodial service

___5 buildings in good repair

___6 furnishings in good repair

___7 emergency exit procedures and training in case of fire or other disasters

___8 compliance with the Americans with Disabilities Act in providing accessibility for the disabled

___9 adequate access to clean restrooms

__10 adequate safety and security procedures, including efficient access to security personnel

___ Other: ___________________

Action Plan/Next Steps

Sample Evidence

__ site inspection reports
__ accreditation reports
__ interviews with faculty and staff
__ compliance reviews
__ other:______________________

Comments

Score

0 1 2 3 NA

Priority

High Low

7. Employment Conditions and Staffing

STAFFING

D. The program recruits and hires qualified instructional staff with training in the theory and methodology of teaching ESL. Qualifications may vary according to local agency requirements and type of instructional position (e.g., paid instructor, volunteer).

Measures

To score a 2 or 3, the following measures should be in place.

___1 The minimum qualifications for teaching in the program include formal training in TESOL. Formal training may include one or more of the following:

- __ master's degree in TESOL
- __ master's degree in linguistics or a related subject with specialization in TESOL
- __ bachelor's degree in TESOL
- __ adult education teaching credential with endorsement or authorization to teach ESL
- __ TESOL certificate from an accredited institution
- __ certificate of completion from provider's preservice TESOL training program
- __ specified amount of experience teaching ESL to adults
- __ progress toward completion of course work for certificate or degree in TESOL
- __ combination of adult-level ESL teaching experience, internship, and training determined to be equivalent

  specify:_______________

___2 The qualifications for teaching are commensurate with those of the institution's other instructional or professional staff.

___ Other:_______________________

Sample Evidence

- __ transcripts from accredited institutions
- __ letters of satisfactory completion of training
- __ certificates of completion from training programs
- __ portfolios with evidence of knowledge and methodology of teaching ESL
- __ hiring guidelines/qualifications
- __ recruitment materials advertising positions
- __ documentation listing the qualifications of the instructional staff currently employed:
  - __ number with a master's degree in TESOL
  - __ number with a master's degree in linguistics or a related subject with specialization in TESOL
  - __ number with a bachelor's degree in TESOL
  - __ number with an adult education teaching credential with endorsement or authorization to teach ESOL
  - __ number with a TESOL certificate from an accredited institution
  - __ number with a certificate of completion from provider's preservice TESOL training program
  - __ number with a specified amount of experience teaching ESOL to adults: number of years required: _____
  - __ number with progress toward completion of course work for certificate or degree in TESOL
  - __ number with a combination of adult-level ESOL teaching experience, internship, and training determined to be equivalent
  - __ other:___________________

Action Plan/Next Steps

Comments

Score

0 1 2 3 NA

Priority

High Low

7. Employment Conditions and Staffing

STAFFING

E. The program recruits and hires qualified administrative, instructional, and support staff who have appropriate training in cross-cultural communication, reflect the cultural diversity of the learners in the program, and have experience with or awareness of the specific needs of adult English learners in their communities.

Measures

To score a 2 or 3, one of the following measures should be in place:

Staff members demonstrate training in cross-cultural communication or reflect the cultural diversity of learners in any one of the following ways:

___1 The staff has experience communicating with nonnative speakers of English through any of the following:
- __ residence or work experience in another country
- __ work experience among a diverse population in the United States
- __ family relationships
- __ other: ___________________

___2 The staff either speak the languages or demonstrate an understanding of the cultures of the dominant learner populations in the program by doing any of the following:
- __ read appropriate literature on the student population
- __ attend community forums or meetings
- __ participate in regular conversations with learners about their lives, needs, and goals
- __ have participated in programs as a learner
- __ complete training sessions or course on cross-cultural communication

___ Other: ___________________

Action Plan/Next Steps

Sample Evidence

- __ resumes of staff
- __ interviews with staff
- __ lists of faculty and staff members describing their prior work experience
- __ portfolios with evidence of cross-cultural communication
- __ hiring guidelines and qualifications
- __ recruitment materials advertising positions
- __ administrative evaluations
- __ administrators' daily calendars
- __ other: ________________________

Comments

Score

0 1 2 3 NA

Priority

High Low

7. Employment Conditions and Staffing

Staffing

F. The program recruits and hires qualified support staff to ensure effective program operation.

Measures

To score a 2 or 3, all the measures should be in place.

___1 Based on the size of the program budget and the needs expressed by the instructional staff, an appropriate number of support people are hired to ensure efficient day-to-day operations. Examples of these staff positions are any of the following:

- __ receptionists
- __ account clerks
- __ attendance clerks
- __ office manager
- __ instructional aides
- __ clerical assistants
- __ technology support technicians or specialists
- __ instructional specialists
- __ student support specialists

___2 The hiring process for support staff ensures appropriate training and qualifications for the job assignments.

___3 Support staff receive an orientation to the goals, structure, and mission of the program.

___4 Support staff are screened for their abilities to work with and support the learner population.

____ Other: ______________________

Action Plan/Next Steps

Sample Evidence

- __ personnel records
- __ list of support staff describing their qualifications or prior work experience
- __ interviews with instructional staff and support staff
- __ observations
- __ recruitment ads and hiring guidelines
- __ staff evaluations
- __ interviews with learners
- __ other: ______________________

Comments

Score

0 1 2 3 NA

Priority

High Low

8. Professional Development and Staff Evaluation

Professional Development

A. The program has a process for orienting new ESL administrative, instructional, and support staff to the ESL program, its goals, and its learners.

Measures

To score a 2 or 3, the following measure should be in place.

____ Orientation is provided in one or more of the following ways:

- __ group workshop
- __ written program descriptions
- __ job shadowing experience
- __ observation of instruction and other program activities
- __ video or other form of presentation to staff
- __ one-to-one discussion with supervisor
- __ other: ________________

Sample Evidence

- __ orientation materials
- __ interviews with staff
- __ observation of orientation process
- __ schedule of orientation activities
- __ other: ________________________

Comments

Action Plan/Next Steps

Score

0 1 2 3 NA

Priority

High Low

8. Professional Development and Staff Evaluation

Professional Development

B. The program has a professional development plan, developed with input from staff and stakeholders. The program acquires appropriate resources to implement the plan, including compensation for staff participation.

Measures

To score a 2 or 3, all the * measures should be in place.

*__1 The program's professional development plan has all the following components:
- __ The plan is based on research in the field.
- __ The plan is based on external influences, such as legislation.
- __ The plan draws on input from internal stakeholders through a staff development needs assessment .
- __ The program conducts a staff development needs assessment on a regular basis. Date of last needs assessment: ________

*__2 The plan has a budget that allocates financial resources to support staff development. Resources may be required to do any of the following:
- __ provide for workshop presenters
- __ compensate faculty and staff to attend training workshops
- __ provide professional growth credits toward salary advancement for those who acquire professional development
- __ fund staff to travel to workshops or conferences
- __ provide release time for faculty and staff to attend in-service training
- __ pay for memberships of staff in professional organizations such as TESOL

__3 The program seeks and acquires supplemental grant funding to provide staff development as outlined in the plan.

*__4 The plan includes a process to evaluate implementation of the plan.

Action Plan/Next Steps

Sample Evidence

__ professional development plan
__ payroll records showing evidence of compensation for staff development activities
__ needs assessment forms
__ program budget
__ grants
__ other: ____________________

Comments

Score

0 1 2 3 NA

Priority

High Low

8. Professional Development and Staff Evaluation

Professional Development

C. The program provides opportunities for its instructional staff to expand their knowledge of current trends, best practices, uses of technology, and research in the field of second language acquisition and adult literacy development.

Measures

To score a 2 or 3, all the measures should be in place.

___1 The program provides opportunities for expansion of knowledge in areas such as the following:

- __ current trends
- __ best practices and methodology
- __ use of technology in ESL
- __ research in second language acquisition
- __ cross-cultural training
- __ knowledge of learners' cultures and languages

___2 The program provides access to up-to-date resources on second language acquisition, teaching methods, and previous course syllabi or outlines, including an up-to-date resource library and technological resources

___ Other:____________________

Sample Evidence

- __ resource library materials
- __ access to Web sites related to ESL
- __ calendar of staff development activities
- __ interviews with staff
- __ subscriptions to ESL publications or periodicals
- __ records of travel to conferences by instructional staff
- __ workshop training materials
- __ other: ____________________

Comments

Action Plan/Next Steps

Score

0 1 2 3 NA

Priority

High Low

8. Professional Development and Staff Evaluation

Professional Development

D. The program provides opportunities for administrators and project evaluators to become knowledgeable about effective teaching strategies in adult ESL and current trends in the field of adult ESL.

Measures

To score a 2 or 3, the following measure should be in place.

___1 The program provides opportunities for administrators and project evaluators to become knowledgeable in one or more of the following ways:

- __ offering training to administrators on effective teaching strategies, especially the criteria for classroom observations
- __ requiring regular dialogue between administrators and instructional staff
- __ encouraging administrators to attend adult-level ESL conferences and workshops
- __ requiring classroom observations of adult ESL teachers followed by discussion between the administrator and teacher
- __ other:___________________

Sample Evidence

- __ workshop training materials
- __ interviews with administrators and staff
- __ records of travel to conferences by administrators and staff
- __ resource library materials
- __ calendar of staff development activities and classroom observations
- __ access to Web sites related to ESL
- __ classroom observation rating sheets with administrators' discussion notes
- __ other: _________________

Comments

Action Plan/Next Steps

Score

0 1 2 3 NA

Priority

High Low

8. Professional Development and Staff Evaluation

Professional Development

E. Professional development activities are varied, based on needs of the staff, and provide opportunities for practice and consistent follow-up.

Measures

To score a 2 or 3, all the measures should be in place.

____1 Professional development activities include a combination of the following:
- __ in-house workshops by staff or outside presenters
- __ invited speakers
- __ training workshops outside the program
- __ credit for course work, including on-line instruction
- __ mentoring projects
- __ action research related to adult-level ESL instruction
- __ peer coaching
- __ shadowing opportunities whereby staff is supported to learn under others
- __ sabbatical leaves
- __ distance-learning opportunities
- __ text and material publication
- __ other: ________________

____2 The program encourages practice and follow-up activities to staff development to monitor implementation of new strategies. Ways to provide follow-up include one or more of the following:
- __ sponsor meetings or workshops in which staff members share with each other what they learned at staff development activities
- __ facilitate classroom observations between staff members to monitor the application of new strategies
- __ publish a newsletter summarizing results or new strategies learned from staff development activities

___ Other: ____________________

Action Plan/Next Steps

Sample Evidence

- __ professional development plan
- __ needs assessment results
- __ interviews with instructional staff
- __ staff development schedule
- __ staff development training materials
- __ records of staff development activities for each instructor
- __ list of invited speakers or workshop presenters
- __ other: ____________________

Comments

Score

0 1 2 3 NA

Priority

High Low

8. Professional Development and Staff Evaluation

Professional Development

F. The program provides training in assessment procedures in the interpretation and use of assessment results.

Measures

To score a 2 or 3, all the measures should be in place.

___1 Training on assessment procedures is provided in any of the following ways:

- __ in house meetings or workshops
- __ invited trainers
- __ supported attendance at outside workshops

___2 Training is provided for a variety of assessment procedures. These may include training in the following:

- __ standardized testing
- __ performance based testing
- __ portfolio based assessment

___3 Training is provided on the following:

- __ purposes of assessment (e.g., for placement, for progress)
- __ appropriate methods of test administration
- __ interpretation and use of test results

___4 For mandated testing, the program supports participation in the training sessions in any of the following ways:

- __ paid compensation
- __ released time from the classroom

___5 All program staff associated with assessment participate in training sessions (e.g., administrators, instructors, and assessment staff).

___ Other: ________________

Action Plan/Next Steps

Sample Evidence

- __ professional development plan
- __ schedule of training meetings or workshops related to assessment
- __ training manuals for instructional and support staff
- __ interviews with instructional staff
- __ observation of trainings
- __ other: ________________

Comments

Score

0 1 2 3 NA

Priority

High Low

8. Professional Development and Staff Evaluation

Professional Development

G. The program encourages faculty and staff to join professional ESL and adult education organizations and supports staff participation in professional development activities of the organizations.

Measures

To score a 2 or 3, one or more of the following measures should be in place.

The program encourages participation in professional organizations in one or more of the following ways:

___1 The program makes available information on professional organizations and encourages membership.

___2 The program encourages and, if possible, compensates staff to participate in staff development activities of the organization, such as

- __ conferences
- __ retreats
- __ intensive training sessions

___3 The program supports staff who present at professional conferences or meetings by providing any of the following:

- __ travel reimbursement
- __ release time
- __ duplication of materials for presentation
- __ payment of conference fees

___4 The program recognizes membership and participation in professional organizations through staff evaluation activities.

____ Other: ____________________

Action Plan/Next Steps

Sample Evidence

- __ record of memberships in ESL organizations by instructional staff
- __ travel requests or travel records by instructional staff
- __ staff development budget
- __ interviews with instructional staff
- __ record of staff presentations at conferences
- __ release-time records
- __ newsletters or program reports that acknowledge staff participation in professional development activities
- __ other: _____________

Comments

Score

0 1 2 3 NA

Priority

High Low

8. Professional Development and Staff Evaluation

Professional Development

H. The program supports collaboration among adult ESL teachers, instructional personnel in other content areas, K–12 English and ESL teachers, support service providers, workplace personnel, and representatives of programs to which students transition.

Measures

To score a 2 or 3, the * measure should be in place.

*__1 The program supports the attendance of its faculty and staff at meetings to collaborate with other educational and community groups, such as

- __ community agencies: __________
- __ K–12 schools: _________
- __ educational oversight and policy groups (e.g., school board)
- __ workplace providers: _________
- __ other segments of own educational program (e.g., adult basic education [ABE] program, graduate equivalency diploma [GED]/high school program, vocational training programs): ____________
- __ colleges: ________________
- __ support service providers: ___________
- __ outside job training programs
- __ business/industries

__2 The program supports the joint use of facilities or resources.

__3 The program provides technological resources and support for joint projects such as the following:

- __ transitioning projects
- __ collaborative learning
- __ research
- __ instructional projects

____ Other: ___________________

Action Plan/Next Steps

Sample Evidence

- __ memorandum of understanding agreements between agencies
- __ meeting notes/agendas
- __ interviews with instructors
- __ grants that require collaboration
- __ reports from collaborative projects
- __ other:

Comments

Score

0 1 2 3 NA

Priority

High Low

8. Professional Development and Staff Evaluation

Professional Development

I. The program has a process for recognizing the participation of staff in professional development activities.

Measures

To score a 2 or 3, the following measure should be in place.

____ The program monitors and recognizes the staff development activities of its staff by doing one or more of the following:

__ awarding certificates of completion or participation in staff development activities
__ recognizing staff development participation in its evaluation procedures for continued employment
__ honoring participants in public ceremonies
__ acknowledging participants in program newsletters, reports, or publicity
__ other:__________________

Sample Evidence

__ sample certificates of recognition or participation
__ newsletter, program reports, or program publicity that acknowledges participation
__ staff evaluation forms
__ ceremony programs/ agenda
__ interviews with staff
__ other: ______________________

Comments

Action Plan/Next Steps

Score

0 1 2 3 NA

Priority

High Low

8. Professional Development and Staff Evaluation

Staff Evaluation

J. The program has a process for the regular evaluation of administrator, instructor, and support staff performance that is consistent with the program's philosophy. The process is developed with input from staff.

K. The program provides learners with opportunities to evaluate program staff anonymously. The tools are user friendly and allow for variety in learner proficiency levels, backgrounds, cultural diversity, and special needs.

L. The program provides opportunities for all staff members to develop performance improvement plans.

Measures for Standards J, K, and L

To score a 2 or 3, all the * measures should be in place.

__1 The staff evaluation instrument and process was developed in collaboration with the instructional staff and approved by all participants.

*__2 The procedures for staff evaluation are clearly defined to all participants in the process

*__3 The evaluation instrument and process are regularly reviewed by all participants and revised as needed.

*__4 Staff evaluations are conducted on a regular basis:

__ once an instructional term
__ once a year
__ every 2 years
__ other: _______________

Continued on p. 139

8. Professional Development and Staff Evaluation

Staff Evaluation

J, K, L. *Continued*

Measures, *continued*

*__5 Multiple measures are used to evaluate performance. At least two of the following measures are used:

- __ classroom observation by administrator
- __ classroom observation by peer instructor
- __ interview with staff member
- __ review of portfolio of instructional materials or curriculum or project developed or participated in by the staff member
- __ survey of learners anonymously
- __ self-evaluation by instructor
- __ other: ____________________

*__6 The outcome of the evaluation process provides an opportunity to improve performance. Formal notice is given of dissatisfaction with faculty performance with a probationary period and guidelines for improvement.

__7 Staff members develop self-improvement plans based on performance evaluations. The self-improvement plan can be completed in any of the following formats, if allowed by program requirements:

- __ interview with administrator or peer instructor
- __ written plan including deadlines and specific objectives
- __ teacher-created format
- __ other:________________

Action Plan/Next Steps

Sample Evidence

- __ staff evaluation forms and guidelines
- __ sample completed staff evaluations
- __ interviews with staff including supervisors or administrators
- __ interviews with students
- __ sample staff evaluation improvement plan
- __ schedule of evaluations, observations, etc.
- __ evaluation forms designed for student use
- __ policy manual or procedural guidelines
- __ documentation of date of last series of staff evaluations:________________
- __ other: ______________________

Comments

Score

0 1 2 3 NA

Priority

High Low

9. Support Services

A. The program provides students with access to a variety of services directly or through referrals to cooperating agencies.

Measures

To score a 2 or 3, all the * measures should be in place.

*__1 The program establishes and maintains contacts with service providers in areas of identified learner needs. The types of services or agencies may include any of the following:

- __ childcare
- __ transportation
- __ health services
- __ employment counseling
- __ educational counseling
- __ financial aide counseling
- __ legal advice
- __ personal and family counseling
- __ assessment of learning disabilities
- __ native language translators
- __ services related to other barriers to learning:________________

__2 When possible, classes are planned in locations where other services such as counseling and health services are available.

*__3 The program maintains an accessible and updated list of experts and agencies for referrals and teacher consultation.

*__4 The program schedules visits from in-house support staff and local representatives from support agencies to talk to learners and staff.

__5 When possible, the program schedules visits by learners to agencies, support services, and other resource locations.

*__6 Instructional and support staff have an understanding of procedures, resources, and responsibilities for providing support to students.

__7 The program provides native-language translation and interpreting through in-house staff or community contacts.

___ Other: ____________________

Action Plan/Next Steps

Sample Evidence

- __ counseling records
- __ memorandum of understanding agreements between agencies
- __ telephone records
- __ program flyers or publicity
- __ learner records showing referrals
- __ list of support services and agencies with contact information
- __ records or schedule of visits to cooperating agencies
- __ records or schedule of visits from/ presentations by agency personnel
- __ program policies and referral guidelines
- __ other:________________________

Comments

Score

0 1 2 3 NA

Priority

High Low

9. Support Services

B. The program provides a process for identifying learning disabilities in English language learners and incorporates appropriate accommodations and training of staff, either directly through the program or indirectly through referrals to cooperating agencies.

Measures

To score a 2 or 3, all the measures should be in place.

__1 The program provides education and training to instructional staff about learning disabilities; types and means of accommodations; appropriate modification of teaching strategies, approaches, and techniques; and referral procedures.

__2 The program arranges for appropriate accommodations, such as any of the following:

- __ modified tables/chairs
- __ note-taking
- __ interpreters
- __ modified instructional materials
- __ assistive technology (e.g., magnification equipment)
- __ assistive staff

__3 Program and instructional staff receive a written description of the procedures for identifying suspected learning disabilities and referral for appropriate diagnosis.

___ Other: ______________

Sample Evidence

- __ list of agencies providing services
- __ written referral process within program
- __ list of available accommodations
- __ interviews with staff
- __ learner records
- __ training agenda
- __ written list of procedures for identifying disabilities
- __ observation or site audit
- __ training materials
- __ other: ____________________

Comments

Action Plan/Next Steps

Score

0 1 2 3 NA

Priority

High Low

9. Support Services

C. The program develops linkages with cooperating agencies to ensure that referrals to support services result in meeting learners' needs, including those of learners with disabilities.

Measures

To score a 2 or 3, one or more of the measures should be in place.

__1 Program staff follow up on referrals made to support agencies to ensure that appropriate services were provided.

__2 Program staff communicate with learners to ensure that needed services were provided.

__3 Program staff investigate the extent to which support agencies accommodate the linguistic and cultural diversity of referred learners.

__4 Written procedures for referrals and identification of learning disabilities include steps for follow up.

__5 If necessary, the program offers information to support agencies to facilitate needed linguistic and cultural accommodations.

__ Other: ________________

Action Plan/Next Steps

Sample Evidence

__ memorandum of understanding agreements between agencies
__ written responses from agencies after referrals
__ interviews with staff
__ interviews with learners
__ summary reports of results of referrals
__ needs assessment
__ records of communication with cooperating agencies, including referrals and follow-up
__ written program policies and procedures
__ other: ________________

Comments

Score

0 1 2 3 NA

Priority

High Low

Summary Scores and Action Plan Chart

Directions: Transfer your program's individual scores for each standard to this chart to analyze the strengths and areas for improvement for each part of your program. Record the proposed steps for improvement in the box titled "Action Plan" at the end of each section. Then under "Priority Areas for Improvement," list the sections and standards that are most in need of improvement, based on the results of this program review.

Scoring Key:

0 — Program component not in place
1 — Program component somewhat in place
2 — Program component in place
3 — Program component in place and well developed
NA — Not applicable to my program or not assessed at this time

1. Program Structure and Administration

Specific Standards	0	1	2	3	NA
A. Mission statement, philosophy, and goals					
B. System of governance					
C. Sound financial procedures					
D. Accountability Plan					
E. Clear communication and linkages with internal and external stakeholders					
F. Procedure for ensuring confidentiality					

G. Equipment for daily operations and efficient record keeping					
H. Appropriate facilities and resources for instruction					
I. Courses of sufficient intensity and duration/ flexible schedules and convenient locations for learners					
J. Student-teacher ratio appropriate to learner needs and goals					
K. (See 2. Standards for Curriculum)					
L. (See 3. Standards for Instruction)					
M. (See 6. Standards for Assessment)					
N. (See 7. Standards for Employment Conditions and Staffing)					

Program Planning

Specific Standards	0	1	2	3	NA
O. Planning process					
P. Technology plan					
Q. Plan for outreach, marketing, and public relations					
Overall Score for Standard Category					

Action Plan

2. Curriculum and Instructional Materials

Specific Standards	0	1	2	3	NA
A. Process for developing curriculum					
B. Compatibility with principles of second language acquisition, mission, and philosophy of program					
C. Goals, objectives, outcomes, approaches, methods, activities, materials, resources, and evaluation measures					
D. Measurable learning objectives					

E. Materials easily accessible, up to date, appropriate for adult learners, suitable for variety of learning styles, culturally sensitive, and oriented to needs of learners					
F. Ongoing process for curriculum revision					
Overall Score for Standard Category					

Action Plan

3. Instruction

Specific Standards	0	1	2	3	NA
A. Activities adhere to adult learning principles and second language acquisition					
B. Varied instructional approaches according to needs of students					
C. Learners take active role in learning process					
D. Focus on acquisition of communication skills					
E. Integration of four language skills					
F. Varied activities according to different learning styles and special learning needs					
G. Variety of grouping strategies and interactive tasks					
H. Activities accommodate multi-level groups of students, especially those with minimal literacy skills					
I. Activities develop language for critical thinking, problem solving, team participation, and study skills					
J. Use of authentic resources					
K. Use of appropriate technologies					
L. Integration of language and culture					
M. Preparation of students for formal and informal assessment					
Overall Score for Standard Category					

Action Plan

4. Learner Recruitment, Intake, and Orientation

Specific Standards	0	1	2	3	NA
A. Effective procedures for identifying adult ESOL learners					
B. Variety of recruitment strategies					
C. Materials reach population in multiple languages as needed					
D. Evaluation of effectiveness of recruitment strategies.					
E. Intake process, orientation to the program, and referral services as needed					
Overall Score for Standard Category					

Action Plan

5. Learner Retention and Transition

Specific Standards	0	1	2	3	NA
A. Enrollment and attendance procedures that support demands on adult learners					
B. Encouragement to reach goals					
C. Accommodation of special needs of learners					
D. Contact with learners with irregular attendance patterns/ acknowledgment of good attendance					
E. Appropriate support for transition to other programs					
Overall Score for Standard Category					

Action Plan

6. Assessment and Learner Gains

Assessment Policy					
Specific Standards	0	1	2	3	NA
A. Assessment policy					
B. Process of assessment for placement, progress, and exit from program					
C. Ongoing assessment and appropriately scheduled					
D. Procedures for collecting and reporting data on gains and outcomes					
E. Appropriate facilities, equipment, supplies, and personnel for assessment					
Types of Assessment					
F. Identification of learners' needs and goals					
G. Assessment of language proficiency levels in listening, speaking, reading, writing, including native language literacy					
H. Variety of assessments including reliable and valid standardized assessment tools					
Uses of Assessment					
I. Assessment information aids curriculum development					
J. Assessment results shared with learners					
K. Assessment documents learners' progress toward advancement to other programs					
L. Results provide information about educational gains and outcomes					
Learner Gains					
M. Process to identify short and long term goals and progress toward attainment of goals					
N. Process to demonstrate skill level improvements in listening, speaking, reading, and writing					
O. Process to demonstrate progress in nonlinguistic areas					
Overall Score for Standard Category					

Action Plan

7. Employment Conditions and Staffing

Specific Standards	0	1	2	3	NA
A. Appropriate compensation and benefits					
B. Professional treatment of staff					
C. Safe and clean working environment					
D. Hiring of qualified instructors trained in ESOL					
E. Hiring of staff with appropriate training in cross-cultural communication					
F. Trained support staff for effective program operation					
Overall Score for Standard Category					

Action Plan

8. Professional Development and Staff Evaluation

Specific Standards	0	1	2	3	NA
A. Orientation for new ESOL administrative, instructional, and support staff					
B. Professional development plan including resources to implement plan					
C. Opportunities to expand knowledge of trends and best practices					
D. Opportunities for administrators/ evaluators to gain knowledge of effective strategies in adult level ESOL					
E. Variety of professional development activities, including practice and follow-up					
F. Training in assessment procedures and use of results					
G. Encouragement to join professional ESOL organizations					
H. Support of collaboration of instructors with other programs					
I. Recognition of participation in professional development activities					

Staff Evaluation

Specific Standards	0	1	2	3	NA
J. Process for regular evaluation of staff					
K. Anonymous evaluation of staff by learners					
L. Opportunity to develop performance improvement plans					
Overall Score for Standard Category					

Action Plan

9. Support Services

Specific Standards	0	1	2	3	NA
A. Access to a variety of services					
B. Process for identifying learning disabilities					
C. Linkages with cooperating agencies					
Overall Score for Section					

Action Plan

Priority Areas for Improvement

Standards Category	Specific Standards

Appendix

Educational Functioning Level Descriptors and Outcome Measure Definitions for English as a Second Language

Literacy Level	**BEGINNING ESL LITERACY** Test benchmark: CASAS (Life Skills): 165–180 SPL (Speaking) 0–1 SPL (Reading and Writing) 0–1 Oral Best: 0–15
Speaking and Listening	Individual cannot speak or understand English, or understands only isolated words or phrases.
Basic Reading and Writing	Individual has no reading or writing skills in any language, or has minimal skills, such as the ability to read and write own name or simple isolated words. The individual may be able to write letters or numbers and copy simple words and there may be no or incomplete recognition of the alphabet; may have difficulty using a writing instrument. There is little or no comprehension of how print corresponds to spoken language.
Functional and Workplace Skills	Individual functions minimally or not at all in English and can communicate only through gestures or a few isolated words, such as name and other personal information; may recognize only common signs or symbols (e.g., stop sign, product logos); can handle only very routine entry-level jobs that do not require oral or written communication in English. There is no knowledge or use of computers or technology.

Literacy Level

Beginning ESL

Test benchmark:
CASAS (Life Skills): 181–200
SPL (Speaking) 2–3
SPL (Reading and Writing) 2–4
Oral Best 16–41

Speaking and Listening

Individual can understand frequently used words in context and very simple phrases spoken slowly and with some repetition; there is little communicative output and only in the most routine situations; little or no control over basic grammar; survival needs can be communicated simply, and there is some understanding of simple questions.

Basic Reading and Writing

Individual can read and print numbers and letters, but has a limited understanding of connected prose and may need frequent rereading; can write sight words and copy lists of familiar words and phrases; may also be able to write simple sentences or phrases such as name, address and phone number; may also write very simple messages. Narrative writing is disorganized and unclear; inconsistently uses simple punctuation (e.g., periods, commas, question marks); contains frequent errors in spelling.

Functional and Workplace Skills

Individual functions with difficulty in situations related to immediate needs and in limited social situations; has some simple oral communication abilities using simple learned and repeated phrases; may need frequent repetition; can provide personal information on simple forms; can recognize common forms of print found in the home and environment, such as labels and product names; can handle routine entry level jobs that require only the most basic written or oral English communication and in which job tasks can be demonstrated. There is minimal knowledge or experience using computers or technology.

Literacy Level	**LOW INTERMEDIATE ESL** Test benchmark: CASAS (Life Skills): 201–210 SPL (Speaking) 4 SPL (Reading and Writing) 5 Oral Best: 42–50
Speaking and Listening	Individual can understand simple learned phrases and limited new phrases containing familiar vocabulary spoken slowly with frequent repetition; can ask and respond to questions using such phrases; can express basic survival needs and participate in some routine social conversations, although with some difficulty; has some control of basic grammar.
Basic Reading and Writing	Individual can read simple material on familiar subjects and comprehend with high accuracy simple and compound sentences in single or linked paragraphs containing a familiar vocabulary; can write simple notes and messages on familiar situations, but lacks complete clarity and focus. Sentence structure lacks variety, but shows some control of basic grammar (e.g., present and past tense), and consistent use of punctuation (e.g., periods, capitalization).
Functional and Workplace Skills	Individual can interpret simple directions and schedules, signs and maps; can fill out simple forms, but needs support on some documents that are not simplified; can handle routine entry level jobs that involve some written or oral English communication, but in which job tasks can be demonstrated. Individual can use simple computer programs and can perform a sequence of routine tasks given directions using technology (e.g., fax machine, computer).

Literacy Level

HIGH INTERMEDIATE ESL

Test benchmark:
CASAS (Life Skills): 211–220
SPL (Speaking) 5
SPL (Reading and Writing) 6
Oral Best: 51–57

Speaking and Listening

Individual can understand learned phrases and short new phrases containing familiar vocabulary spoken slowly and with some repetition; can communicate basic survival needs with some help; can participate in conversation in limited social situations and use new phrases with hesitation; relies on description and concrete terms. There is inconsistent control of more complex grammar.

Basic Reading and Writing

Individual can read text on familiar subjects that have a simple and clear underlying structure (e.g., clear main idea, chronological order); can use context to determine meaning; can interpret actions required in specific written directions, can write simple paragraphs with main idea and supporting detail on familiar topics (e.g., daily activities, personal issues) by recombining learned vocabulary and structures; can self and peer edit for spelling and punctuation errors.

Functional and Workplace Skills

Individual can meet basic survival and social needs, can follow some simple oral and written instruction and has some ability to communicate on the telephone on familiar subjects; can write messages and notes related to basic needs; complete basic medical forms and job applications; can handle jobs that involve basic oral instructions and written communication in tasks that can be clarified orally. The individual can work with or learn basic computer software, such as word processing; can follow simple instructions for using technology.

Literacy Level

Low Advanced ESL

Test benchmark:
CASAS (Life Skills): 221–235
SPL (Speaking) 6
SPL (Reading and Writing) 7
Oral Best 58–64

Speaking and Listening

Individual can converse on many everyday subjects and some subjects with unfamiliar vocabulary, but may need repetition, rewording or slower speech; can speak creatively, but with hesitation; can clarify general meaning by rewording and has control of basic grammar; understands descriptive and spoken narrative and can comprehend abstract concepts in familiar contexts.

Basic Reading and Writing

Individual is able to read simple descriptions and narratives on familiar subjects or from which new vocabulary can be determined by context; can make some minimal inferences about familiar texts and compare and contrast information from such texts, but not consistently. The individual can write simple narrative descriptions and short essays on familiar topics, such as customs in native country; has consistent use of basic punctuation, but makes grammatical errors with complex structures.

Functional and Workplace Skills

Individual can function independently to meet most survival needs and can communicate on the telephone on familiar topics; can interpret simple charts and graphics; can handle jobs that require simple oral and written instructions, multi-step diagrams and limited public interaction. The individual can use all basic software applications, understand the impact of technology and select the correct technology in a new situation.

Literacy Level

HIGH ADVANCED ESL

Test benchmark:
CASAS (Life Skills): 236 and above
SPL (Speaking) 7 and higher
SPL (Reading and Writing) 8 and higher
Oral Best 65 and higher

Speaking and Listening

Individual can understand and participate effectively in face-to-face conversations on everyday subjects spoken at normal speed; can converse and understand independently in survival, work and social situations; can expand on basic ideas in conversation, but with some hesitation; can clarify general meaning and control basic grammar, although still lacks total control over complex structures.

Basic Reading and Writing

Individual can read authentic materials on everyday subjects and can handle most reading related to life roles; can consistently and fully interpret descriptive narratives on familiar topics and gain meaning from unfamiliar topics; uses increased control of language and meaning-making strategies to gain meaning of unfamiliar texts. The individual can write multiparagraph essays with a clear introduction and development of ideas; writing contains well formed sentences, appropriate mechanics and spelling, and few grammatical errors.

Functional and Workplace Skills

Individual has a general ability to use English effectively to meet most routine social and work situations; can interpret routine charts, graphs and tables and complete forms; has high ability to communicate on the telephone and understand radio and television; can meet work demands that require reading and writing and can interact with the public. The individual can use common software and learn new applications; can define the purpose of software and select new applications appropriately; can instruct others in use of software and technology.

From: National Reporting System (n.d.)

References and Further Reading

Alberta Teachers of English as a Second Language. (1995). *Best practice guidelines for adult ESL/LINC programming and instruction in Alberta.* Calgary, Alberta, Canada: Author.

Association for Community Based Education Evaluation and Training Project. (1993). *Framework for assessing program quality.* Washington, DC: Association for Community Based Education.

Brown, H. D. (1994). *Teaching by principles.* Englewood Cliffs, NJ: Prentice Hall Regents.

Burt, M., & Cunningham Florez, M. (2001). *ESL learners in ABE classes.* Washington, DC: National Center for ESL Literacy Education. Available from the NCLE Web site http://www.cal.org/ncle/digests/beginQA.htm

California Department of Education. (1994). *English as a second language quality indicators for adult education programs.* Sacramento, CA: Adult Education Policy and Planning Unit.

Collier, V. P. (1989). How long? A synthesis of research on academic achievement in a second language. *TESOL Quarterly, 23,* 509–531.

Committee on Indicators of Program Quality of New York. (1996). *Looking at literacy: Indicators of program quality.* New York: New York Adult Education and Training Alliance.

Comprehensive Adult Student Assessment System. (1999). *Student progress and goal attainment in California's federally funded ABE program.* San Diego, CA: Author.

Comprehensive Adult Student Assessment System. (2000). *Continuous improvement measure (CIM).* San Diego, CA: Author.

Comprehensive Adult Student Assessment System. (2002). *CASAS resource catalog 2002: Assessment training resources.* San Diego, CA: Author.

Condelli, L. C., & Wrigley, H. S. (2001, September). *"What works" research study.* Paper presented at the National Symposium on Adult ESL Research and Practice, September 5–7, Washington, DC. Retrieved August 12, 2002, from http://www.cal.org/ncle/millenium.htm

Cunningham Florez, M., & Burt, M. (2001). *Beginning to work with adult English language learners: Some considerations.* Washington, DC: National Center for ESL Literacy Education. Retrieved August 12, 2002, from http://www.cal.org/ncle/digests/beginQA.htm

Ellis, R. (1994). *The study of second language acquisition.* New York: Oxford University Press.

Fitzgerald, N. B. (1995). *ESL instruction in adult education: Findings from a national evaluation* (ERIC Digest). Washington, DC: National Center for ESL Literacy Education, Center for Applied Linguistics. Retrieved August 12, 2002, from http://www.cal.org/ncle/digests/fitzgera.htm

Grognet, A. G. (1997). *Performance-based curricula and outcomes: The Mainstream English Language Training Project (MELT) updated for the 1990s and beyond.* Denver, CO: Spring Institute for International Studies ELT.

H.R. 1385, 105th Cong., 2nd Sess. (Workforce Investment Act of 1998, Title II, Adult Education and Family Literacy, Section 203, Definitions, No. 12, Pub. L. No. 105-220). Retrieved February 29, 2000, from http://thomas.loc.gov/cgi-bin/bdquery/z?d105:HR01385:|TOM:/bss/d105query.htm

Isserlis, J. (2000). *Trauma and the adult English language learner.* Washington, DC: National Center for ESL Literacy Education. Retrieved August 12, 2002, from http://www.cal.org/ncle/digests/trauma2.htm

Kim, K., Collins, M., & McArthur, E. (1997). *Participation of adults in English as a second language classes: 1994–95.* Washington, DC: National Center for Education Statistics.

Laubach Literacy Action. (1996). *National quality standards for volunteer literacy programs.* Syracuse, NY: Author.

Mansoor, I. (1992). *Indicators of program quality: An ESL programming perspective.* Arlington, VA: Arlington Education and Employment Program.

Massachusetts Interagency Literacy Group. (1990). *Principles for effective literacy and basic skills programs.* Boston: Author.

National Center for ESL Literacy Education. (1998). *Research agenda for adult ESL.* Washington, DC: Center for Applied Linguistics. Retrieved August 12, 2002, from http://www.cal.org/ncle/agenda

National Center for ESL Literacy Education. (1999). *Frequently asked questions in adult ESL literacy.* Retrieved August 12, 2002, from http://www.cal.org/ncle/faqs.htm

National Center for Family Literacy. (1999). *Strengthening family literacy: How states can increase funding and improve quality.* Washington, DC: National Institute for Literacy.

National Institute for Literacy. (2001, August). *English literacy and civics education for adult learners: Special policy update.* Washington, DC: Author.

National Reporting System. (n.d.). Educational functioning level descriptors and outcome measure definitions for ABE & ESL. Retrieved April 24, 2002, from http://www.air.org/nrs/reports/handouts.pdf

Nunan, D. (1999). *Second language teaching and learning.* Boston: Heinle & Heinle.

Office of Vocational and Adult Education. (2000, March). *Fact sheet 3: Adult education for limited English proficient adults.* Washington, DC: U.S. Department of Education. Retrieved August 12, 2002, from http://www.ed.gov/offices/OVAE/AdultEd/InfoBoard/fact-3.html

Office of Vocational and Adult Education. (1992). *Model indicators of program quality for adult education programs.* Washington, DC: U.S. Department of Education.

O'Malley, J. M., & Chamot, A. U. (1990). *Learning strategies in second language acquisition.* New York: Cambridge University Press.

Oregon Office of Community College Services. (1989). *Indicators of program quality—State plan amendment, Oregon state plan for adult education and literacy, 1989–1990.* Salem, OR: Author.

Schwarz, R., & Terrill, L. (2000). *ESL instruction and adults with learning disabilities.* Washington, DC: National Center for ESL Literacy Education. Retrieved August 12, 2002, from http://www.cal.org/ncle/digests/ld2.htm

Staff Development Institute. (1996). *Programs of excellence: A tool for self review and identification of programs of best practice.* Sacramento: California Department of Education.

Stein, S. (1997). *Equipped for the future: A reform agenda for adult literacy and lifelong learning.* Washington, DC: National Institute for Literacy.

Terrill, L. (2000). *Civics education for adult English language learners.* Washington, DC: National Center for ESL Literacy Education. Retrieved August 12, 2002, from http://www.cal.org/ncle/digests/civics.htm

Tuijnman, A. (2000, September). *Benchmarking adult literacy in America: An international comparative study.* Washington, DC: U.S. Department of Education, Office of Vocational and Adult Education. Retrieved August 12, 2002, from http://www.ed.gov/offices/OVAE/AdultEd/InfoBoard/monograph.pdf

Valentine, T. (1990). *What motivates non-English-speaking adults to participate in the federal English-as-a-Second-Language Program* (Research on Adult Basic Education No. 2). Washington, DC: U.S. Department of Education.

Wrigley, H. S. (1993). *Adult ESL literacy: Findings from a national study*. Washington, DC: National Center for ESL Literacy Education, Center for Applied Linguistics. Retrieved August 12, 2002, from http://www.cal.org/ncle/digests/adult_esl.html

Also Available From TESOL

Action Research
Julian Edge, Editor

Academic Writing Programs
Ilona Leki, Editor

Bilingual Education
Donna Christian and Fred Genesee, Editors

CALL Environments: Research, Practice, and Critical Issues
Joy Egbert and Elizabeth Hanson-Smith, Editors

Community Partnerships
Elsa Auerbach, Editor

Distance-Learning Programs
Lynn E. Henrichsen, Editor

English for Specific Purposes
Thomas Orr, Editor

Internet for English Teaching
Mark Warschauer, Heidi Shetzer, and Christine Meloni

Journal Writing
Jill Burton and Michael Carroll, Editors

Mainstreaming
Effie Cochran, Editor

Reading and Writing in More Than One Language: Lessons for Teachers
Elizabeth Franklin, Editor

Teacher Education
Karen E. Johnson, Editor

Teaching in Action: Case Studies From Second Language Classrooms
Jack C. Richards, Editor

Technology-Enhanced Learning Environments
Elizabeth Hanson-Smith, Editor

For more information, contact

Teachers of English to Speakers of Other Languages, Inc.
700 South Washington Street, Suite 200
Alexandria, Virginia 22314 USA
Tel 703-836-0774 • Fax 703-836-6447 • publications@tesol.org • http://www.tesol.org/